Riga

THE BRADT CITY GUIDE

Stephen Baister
Chris Patrick

Bradt Travel Guides Ltd, UK
The Globe Pequot Press Inc, USA

First published January 2005
Reprinted with amendments August 2005

Bradt Travel Guides Ltd
23 High Street, Chalfont St Peter, Bucks SL9 9QE, England; www.bradtguides.com
Published in the USA by The Globe Pequot Press Inc, 246 Goose Lane, PO Box 480,
Guilford, Connecticut 06437-0480

A catalogue record for this book is available from the British Library
ISBN-10: 1 84162 111 0   ISBN-13: 978 1 84162 111 1

Cover Blackheads' House (Tricia Hayne)
Text photographs Stephen Baister & Chris Patrick (SC), Tricia Hayne (TH), Rachel Russell (RR),
Mark Wadlow (MW)
Maps Steve Munns   *Illustrations* Carole Vincer, Dave Colton

Typeset from the authors' disc by Wakewing
Printed and bound in Italy by Legoprint SpA, Trento

Authors

Stephen Baister studied modern languages at Oxford and London universities and worked as a publisher before becoming a solicitor. While in practice, he represented a number of clients with interests in eastern and central Europe. He was co-author of the *Bradt Guide to East Germany*, published in 1990, and a contributor to *Eastern Europe by Rail* (Bradt Travel Guides, 1994). He has a doctorate in East European law from University College London. He is now a Registrar in Bankruptcy in the High Court.

Chris Patrick has a degree in French and German from Oxford University. After graduation she lived and worked in Japan and travelled extensively in the Far East. She works now in international research and consultancy and has assisted a number of organisations from Eastern Europe in doing business in the Far East. She first visited Latvia in 1989 and has returned many times since. She was co-author of the *Bradt Guide to East Germany*, published in 1990, and a contributor to Bradt's *Eastern Europe by Rail*.

By the same authors: *Latvia: The Bradt Travel Guide*

Baltic Holidays

Since starting out as Lithuanianholidays.com in 2000, we have branched out to become Baltic Holidays, a specialist tour operator to the Baltic States of Lithuania, Latvia & Estonia.

Specialists in:
- City breaks to Vilnius, Riga & Tallinn
- Baltic Tours and country tours
- Tailor-made travel throughout the Baltics
- Family holidays
- City & Spa breaks
- City & Coast breaks
- Family research

Why use us ..?
- We are the only specialist UK travel company to deal solely with the Baltic States
- We visit Lithuania, Latvia & Estonia regularly
- Regular updates with our hotels and suppliers
- Up to date information on the best places to go
- We are fully ATOL bonded, ABTA bonded and members of AITO.

"Our travel through the Baltic States with your company went without a hitch and your wealth of local knowledge ensured we saw most of what there was to see and gain a rewarding insight to these wonderful countries."

Mr & Mrs South, tailor-made Baltic trip, May 03

Go with the leaders not the followers. You won't be disappointed.

Contact details:
Baltic Holidays, 40 Princess Street, Manchester M1 6DE
Tel: 0870 757 9233 Fax: 0870 120 2973
info@balticholidays.com www.balticholidays.com

Contents

Contents

Contents

Acknowledgements

The authors would like to thank Neil Taylor, Director of Regent Holidays, for his invaluable comments on some of Riga's many hotels, restaurants and museums, and also for his help with up-to-date travel information. Many thanks also to Frances Samuel for permission to use her account of the re-opening of the embassy in Riga in 1991.

FEEDBACK

This is a small guide to a large and constantly changing city. If you discover something new or different in Riga, we should be very pleased to hear about it. You can contact us directly at chris_patrick@hotmail.com, or via Bradt Travel Guides, 19 High Street, Chalfont St Peter, Bucks SL9 9QE, England; email: info@bradtguides.com.

Introduction

On May 1 2004 Latvia, along with the other two Baltic states, Estonia and Lithuania, became a member of the European Union. Despite this, the country and its capital, Riga, remain little known. 'Where exactly is that?' is a common response to the statement 'I've just been to Riga'. Although this is not surprising, given the history and size of the country, it is a great pity, as Riga has a huge amount to offer. Not only is it a World Heritage site, because of its historic centre, its art nouveau buildings and its 19th-century wooden architecture, it is also a very enjoyable place just to be. My guess is that within five years the attractions of Riga as a weekend destination will have become much more widely known and appreciated, as more flights become available and visitors report to friends on the wonderful time they have had. Now, then, is the time to go and discover for yourself what makes Riga such a fascinating city.

A sign in the middle of the Old Town in Riga points one way to Moscow (1,011km) and the other way to Berlin (1,226km). Despite the fact that Moscow is slightly nearer and that Latvia was under Soviet occupation as recently as 1991, visitors to Riga today will see almost nothing to remind them of these links. Riga has a distinctly western European feel: a lively centre, full of cafés and bars, a largely restored Old Town, spectacular art nouveau buildings, a wealth of museums and new shopping, entertainment and business centres.

One of the things that makes Riga so interesting is that the more you dig below the surface the more you find. The Soviet occupation, though its effects are now largely invisible, is not forgotten, as a visit to the Occupation Museum or a glance up at the Academy of Sciences ('Stalin's birthday cake') illustrate. Dig further, and you will find grim reminders of the Nazi occupation, relics of the long period of Russian rule from 1710 to World War I, including the palace at Rundāle, easily visitable from Riga, and further back still of the even longer period of German dominance when many of Riga's most imposing buildings, including the Dome Cathedral and St Peter's Church, were erected.

Before all these layers of history built up, however, the area where Riga now stands was inhabited by various Baltic and Finno-Ugrian tribes, the forebears of many present-day Latvians. These people, living close to nature and depending on the river and sea as well as the land, remarkably survived the many different governments which ruled them over the centuries, and in the course of the 19th century gradually forged a strong feeling of national identity which led to independence from 1920 to 1940 and then again from 1991. Evidence of this distinctly Latvian identity is all over Riga. Despite urban growth, a staggering 19% of the city's area consists of parks and gardens and another 16% of rivers, lakes and canals. Flower sellers are everywhere. Folk singing, an artificially preserved art in many countries, continues to attract huge crowds at the Mežaparks with its stage for 20,000 singers. Traditional Latvian cooking is easy to find and enjoy in Riga, and if you visit at the end of June you will experience for yourself midsummer revelry based on centuries-old traditions.

None of this means that Riga is stuck in the past. Over the last few years Riga has been striving with some success to resume its earlier role not only as the largest but also the most cosmopolitan city in the Baltics. It is building on its musical and artistic traditions and putting on more festivals and exhibitions. It is trying to attract international business with ultra-modern buildings and up-to-date facilities. Economically there is some way to go for the majority of the population but, as the cafés and clubs increasingly crowded with young Latvians attest, the future for many now looks brighter than it has for some considerable time.

How to use this book

Email addresses Where one is given, assume that correspondence in English is fine.

Currency The Latvian currency is the lat. You will see it denoted in various ways (eg: Ls5, 5Ls or LS5). In this book we have used Ls5.

Map references (eg: [2 B4]) These relate to the colour map section at the end of the guide.

Names and spelling In general the spellings used in this guide are native Latvian ones. In the case of people's names this means adding an 's' to all male names and an 'a' to all female ones. Because nouns decline, noun endings vary according to context; do not be misled into thinking that slightly different names refer to two different people or places (eg: Raiņa bulvāris is the boulevard named after Latvia's best-known poet, Rainis).

Opening hours An increasing number of cafés open from 08.00 for breakfast (page 83). Others open from 10.00 or so. Some stay open until late in the evening, although others, particularly those which do not serve alcohol, tend to close at 17.00 or 18.00. Restaurants open at 12.00 and do not usually close during the afternoon. Their closing times vary enormously: some stay open until late, so you should always find somewhere to eat, but others close relatively early, so if you have a particular place in mind for an evening meal it is as well to check the closing time. Some restaurants close on Sundays. Bookings are rarely necessary.

Most museums close at least one day a week, and some close for two days. Generally this is Monday and/or Tuesday. They open around 10.00 and close around 17.00, although in the summer months some of the major museums have one night of late opening. Some museums close on national holidays, although pre-booked groups can often arrange for museums to be opened specially for them.

Prices Hotel prices always fluctuate wildly according to the booking agency used, the time of year and the day of the week. Take those listed only as a rough indication.

Restaurant prices always include VAT but rarely service. It is now normal practice to add a 10% tip for good service.

RIGA AT A GLANCE

Location Between Lithuania to the south, Estonia to the north and Russia and Belarus to the east. Riga, its capital, lies on the Gulf of Riga, around 2½ hours' flight from London.

Population 739,232 (almost one-third of the total population of Latvia)

Language Officially Latvian. Russian is also widely spoken. There is no problem in getting by in English.

Religion Predominantly Lutheran, but some Roman Catholics and Russian Orthodox

Time GMT/BST +2

International telephone code +371

Currency Lat (Ls or LS) €1=Ls0.68 (November 2004)

Electricity 220v; two-pin plugs

Public holidays January 1, Good Friday, Easter Monday, May 1, June 23 (Līgo Holiday), June 24 (Midsummer's Day – Jāņi), November 18 (Independence Day), December 25 & 26, December 31

Climate Mild summers, cold winters. Average temperature in July: 18°C. Average temperature in January: –3°C. For weather forecasts, check on-line services such as www.wunderground.com/global/stations/26422.html

Contents

HISTORY

In 2001 Riga celebrated 800 years of recorded history. In all these years Riga has been the capital of an independent country, presided over by Latvians, for a mere 35 years: for 20 years between 1920 and 1940 and again since 1991. The remainder of the time it has been fought over and ruled by peoples from all over northern Europe, but predominantly by the Germans and Russians. What is remarkable is that while other peoples have disappeared or been swallowed up into larger states, a people known as the Latvians have survived to establish themselves with a distinct national identity and their own government and to emerge into the 21st century as an independent nation with Riga as its capital.

Early days

Archaeological excavations indicate that the area now occupied by Riga was probably inhabited and operated as a trading centre as early as the 2nd century BC or even well before: it is thought that the name Riga may originate from a local word *'ringa'*, meaning a winding river, and it is clear that well before 1201 Riga was already developing as a small harbour. The first mention of the modern city can however be traced to 1201 when Bishop Albert von Buxhoevden (or Buksherden) of Bremen established the first German fortress here as part of his crusade to introduce Christianity to the local Livs. Religious life was quickly established, with several churches, including the Dome

Cathedral, founded in the early years of German domination. During the 13th century Riga suffered from no fewer than five major fires, which eventually gave rise to a law prohibiting the construction of wooden houses inside the town walls, but overall the town prospered as a trading centre, joining the Hanseatic League in 1282. Despite the prosperity, there was constant tension between the citizens and their rulers, giving rise to numerous battles and reprisals.

The Reformation

In 1521 St Peter's Church began to operate as a centre for Reformation doctrine; in 1524 the first Latvian Evangelical Lutheran congregation was formed at St James' Church. As Lutheran teachings gained a foothold in Riga, Catholicism retreated: Catholic churches were demolished, and religious paintings and carvings were destroyed. Lutheranism has been the dominant religion ever since. Teutonic influence gradually waned and in 1561 Riga fell into the hands of the Polish/Lithuanian Empire. The end of the 16th century marked a period of instability, and Russia (under Ivan the Terrible), Poland, Denmark and Sweden all laid claim to the city.

17th and 18th centuries

The Polish–Swedish War of 1599–1629 ended as far as Riga was concerned when the city fell to Gustavus Adolphus II in 1621. Following the Peace of Oliva of 1660, Riga became the second capital of Sweden. Again there was a period of commercial success and prosperity. In 1663 a water supply was established using wooden pipes.

In 1681 Riga's first newspaper, the *Rigische Nouvellen*, was established. In 1685 the first Bible was printed in Latvian. In the same year a number of large rocks that blocked navigation of the Daugava were removed by explosion. In 1701 a pontoon bridge was built over the Daugava – it was the longest in the world.

Swedish rule continued until 1710, when after an eight-month siege by the Russians, Riga surrendered to the Russian general, Count Sheremetyer. For the next 200 years Riga remained under Russian control, although it continued to be heavily dominated by the Baltic Germans who lived throughout most of Latvia. This period was by no means a bad one for Riga. Peter I married the fourth daughter of Ernst Glück, the Lutheran pastor who translated the Bible into Latvian. She became Catherine I of Russia. Writing in German of the time he spent in Riga between 1764 and 1789 Johann Gottfried Herder (see page 118) wrote 'I lived, taught and behaved in such a free and such an unrestrained way in Livonia such that I can hardly imagine living and behaving again.' In 1743 street lighting was introduced. In 1782 a theatre was established (where Wagner conducted from 1837–39). Riga was also a place of intellectual and scientific enlightenment in the 18th century. In 1798 Dr Otto Herr introduced vaccination against smallpox, and in 1802 the Latvian pharmacist Grindels founded the Society of Pharmacy, which started a trend for the formation of a whole range of medical and scientific associations. In 1801 torture was abolished as part of the legal process, as was public execution.

The 18th century also saw a growth of Latvian cultural awareness. Whilst Herder wrote his *Fragmente über die neuere deutsche Literatur (Fragments Concerning Recent*

German Literature) in Riga, in 1774 he published a number of Latvian folk songs in German translation.

19th century

Riga avoided the effects of the Napoleonic Wars; although Napoleon had threatened to attack 'this suburb of London', he never reached it. As Napoleon's troops approached Riga in 1812, the governor-general of Riga set the wooden houses of the Riga suburbs on fire to deflect the invaders. In the wake of the French Revolution, the wave of liberation that swept across Europe made itself felt in Riga too, and in 1817 serfs were emancipated, 40 years before those in Russia. In 1830 farmers gained the right to live in the cities. In 1840 a rural education law was passed. Soon an educated rural class grew up, starting up trade in Riga and other towns. Jews were only given residency rights in Riga in the mid-19th century, before which most were itinerant traders. By the outbreak of World War I in 1914, their numbers in Riga had reached about 100,000 and they were active both in commerce and in the academic world.

In 1857–58 the town walls were dismantled to allow expansion. In 1861 the railway came and the postal service was expanded. Riga gradually developed into a major industrial centre and the first shipyard opened in 1869. Telephones arrived in 1877; horse-drawn trams appeared, and a major bicycle factory was established. In 1887 an electric power generation station was built. This industrialisation also brought a huge increase in the population of Riga: in 1767 the town had 16,300 inhabitants; 100 years later the population had grown to 102,590 (of whom about 20–25% were Latvian). By 1897 the population doubled to 255,879, but the Latvian population now accounted for almost 50%. A prosperous Latvian working class and middle class began to emerge.

Parallel to this industrial expansion came a growth in Latvian nationalism. Latvian newspapers, notably *Tas Ļatviešu Ļaužu Draugs* (The Friend of the Latvian People), had appeared since the 1820s and 1830s, but Russian remained the language of education, government and the legal system. However, Krišjāņis Barons' work in collecting Latvia's *dainas*, traditional four-line folksongs, and the establishment of a folk song festival in Riga in 1873 gave impetus to the movement called the Latvian Awakening, which grew out of the Riga Latvian Association. The Latvian Association published a Latvian encyclopedia, founded a national opera and a national theatre. The folk song festival gave birth to a national anthem, *Dievs Svēti Latviju* (God Bless Latvia).

Riot and revolution

The end of the 19th century was also a time of growing working-class political awareness. In 1899 women workers at the Džuta textile mill went on strike. The police intervened, and before long demonstrations began in the course of which five workers were shot dead and 31 wounded. A full-scale riot soon ensued. In 1904 the Latvian Social Democratic Party was formed, the most significant movement of its kind in imperial Russia.

FIVE FAMOUS 20TH-CENTURY RIGANS
Isaiah Berlin (born in Riga in 1909)
The political philosopher Isaiah Berlin lived in Riga at 2a Alberta iela (see page 127) until 1915. His adult life was spent in Britain, where he was a fellow of All Souls College and the first President of Wolfson College, Oxford. He died in Oxford in 1997.

Gunars Birkerts (born in Riga in 1925)
Highly respected architect, resident in the USA since 1949. Major projects include the Federal Reserve Bank in Minneapolis, the Corning Museum of Glass and the IBM Building in Southfield. His plans for a new national library in Riga, to be known as Gaišmaspils ('the castle of light'), have been awaiting funding for several years.

Valters Caps – also known as Walter Zapp (born in Riga in 1905)
Caps invented the Minox camera, the tiny camera used by spies, real and

On January 13 1905 a demonstration of the poor and working classes was put down with force in Moscow. The demonstrators had wanted to show solidarity with demonstrators who had gathered four days earlier in front of the tsar's palace in St Petersburg to hand in a petition seeking political reform. A demonstration in support imaginary, including Sean Connery as James Bond in *You Only Live Twice*. The cameras were made in Latvia from 1938 to 1943. Zapp, who subsequently lived in the USA, died at the age of 97 in 2003.

Mariss Jansons (born in Riga in 1943)

Known to classical music fans throughout the world as a conductor of intensity and imagination. Has worked as Music Director of the Oslo Philharmonic Orchestra and of the Pittsburgh Symphony Orchestra and now conducts the Royal Concertgebouw Orchestra in Amsterdam and the Bavarian Radio Symphony Orchestra in Munich.

Mihails Tāls (born in Riga in 1936)

Known as the Magician of Riga because of his legendary tactical skills, Mihails won the World Chess Championship in 1960 at the age of 24, the second-youngest Chess World Champion of all time. He died in Riga in 1992. In 2001 a monument to the chess player was erected in Vermānes Park.

also began in Riga, but again it was put down by force of arms and over 70 people were killed. The Social Democratic Party began to organise resistance, and by October Riga was in the grip of a general strike. Armed peasants attacked German landowners, and other strikers attacked the prison, aiming to free a number of political prisoners.

Before the end of the year Russian troops moved to regain control, putting the revolution down with particular brutality in which over 900 peasants and teachers were executed under martial law, and thousands were exiled to Siberia. The Russian authorities aimed their vengeance especially at teachers who were known for their social-democratic leanings. Many Latvian intellectuals only escaped by fleeing to the West. The writer, Jānis Rainis, fled to Switzerland, Kārlis Ulmanis, the chairman of the peasants' party, who was later to become president of Latvia, sought refuge in the United States.

World war and the aftermath

The outbreak of World War I drove Latvia into the arms of the Russians with whom they allied themselves against the German foe. In 1915 German forces were approaching Riga. In a manic evacuation, the Russians moved Riga's industry and about 96,000 workers to Russia. Even the power station was dismantled and moved. In all, about one-third of the total population of Latvia was forced to leave the country. In 1917 German troops crossed the Daugava, and the capital surrendered to the Germans.

In the same year, however, the Russian Revolution was making its consequences felt. Whilst some political elements in Riga sought the annexation of Latvia to the German Empire, others were looking to Soviet power to free their country from the Germans. In spring 1918 Latvia was split into three: Kurzeme and Riga went to Germany, Latgale to Russia, and the rest of Vidzeme was left unmolested. However, following the defeat of Germany, on November 18 1918, in the Riga national theatre an independent republic of Latvia was proclaimed, and Kārlis Ulmanis was given the task of forming a provisional government. A period of what amounted to civil war ensued, the Russians supporting Latvia against the persistent exercise of German military force. Only on August 11 1920 was a peace treaty signed between Latvia and the Soviet Union following the final expulsion of German troops from Latvia in December 1919.

The period between the two world wars is often referred to as the first period of Latvian independence. The 1920 treaty provided for the Soviet Union and Latvia to recognise each other as states. In 1922 Latvia adopted its own constitution and issued its own currency. Jānis Čakste was elected as the first president of the republic.

Riga was not immune to the depression that gripped most of Europe during the 1930s and unemployment rose to high levels. On May 15 1934 Ulmanis mounted a coup and formed an authoritarian administration. Democratic socialists were imprisoned, political parties of both left and right were banned, and freedom of the press was curtailed. In 1935, the Freedom Monument was erected in the centre of Riga (page 181).

Under the terms of the pact between Hitler and Stalin of August 23 1939 it was agreed that the Baltic states would fall under the sphere of influence of the Soviet Union. By the end of that year the Soviet Union had already begun to establish a military presence in Latvia. On June 17 1940 Soviet troops marched in to take over the country and establish a pro-Soviet regime. On July 21 'elections' were held under Soviet auspices and a new government and parliament declared Latvia to be

History

a republic of the USSR. Ulmanis was deported, as were thousands of citizens from Riga and elsewhere in Latvia, many of them to Siberia or central Asia.

In June 1941 the USSR was forced to join in the war when attacked by Germany. Latvia was unprepared, and on July 1 1941 Hitler's troops arrived in Riga to 'liberate' it from Stalin's USSR, causing the Soviets to retreat, leaving devastation in their wake. Stalin had murdered or deported a substantial proportion of the Jewish population in Riga as enemies of the people; Hitler imposed his anti-Semitic policies, massacring Jews at Rumbula and Biķernieki, and establishing concentration camps. Riga was 'liberated' on October 13 1944. The German occupation of Kurzeme continued until May 1945 when the Red Army arrived again to 'liberate' Riga from the Germans. The retreating Germans destroyed houses, factories, roads and bridges, and thousands of Latvians fled to the West.

After the end of World War II the USSR provided economic assistance to Latvia, and Russian immigrants took the places left by the fleeing or slaughtered native Latvian population. However, the Soviet 'liberators' were not welcomed: many Latvians formed resistance groups and fighting ensued until Stalin intervened with his usual brutality, ordering mass deportations to Siberia in 1949 and acts of destruction including the blowing up of the Blackheads' House (see page 149) in May 1948.

However, Latvian nationalism whilst repressed was not extinguished. In 1988 5,000 demonstrators gathered in Riga on June 14 to commemorate the deportations, and on August 23 10,000 demonstrators gathered to mark the anniversary of the Hitler–Stalin pact. In the meantime in June at a meeting of the

Latvian Writers' Union a resolution was passed that led to the founding of the Popular Front of Latvia in October 1988 that was to campaign for political, cultural and economic independence.

Liberation and independence

In 1989 Latvia experienced its first free elections of deputies to the Supreme Soviet of the USSR. This event was followed by the passing of laws in the Latvian Supreme Soviet proclaiming the sovereignty of the Latvian Soviet Socialist Republic and declaring Latvian the official language of the country. Latvia was again on the road to independence. On November 18 1989 over 500,000 people gathered on the banks of the Daugava in Riga to mark the 71st anniversary of Latvia's independence.

On May 4 1990 the Supreme Soviet of Latvia met in the pre-war Saeima building and passed a resolution on 'the renewal of Independence of the Republic of Latvia'.

A period of instability followed as the Latvian Communist party endeavoured to take back the helm of government, staging a failed coup in January 1991 in which five people were killed. A plebiscite held in March 1991 resulted in three-quarters of the population voting to secede from the Soviet Union. On August 19 and 20 Soviet troops blocked roads leading to Riga and seized the Interior Ministry building. The Moscow coup failed, however, and on August 21 the Latvian parliament voted to restore independence. On August 25 1991 Iceland became the first country to recognise the new independent Baltic state, but others soon followed, and by the end of the year the Republic of Latvia had been granted admission to the UN. A new constitution proclaiming Latvia as an independent democratic republic was adopted in 1992. Riga was once more the capital of an independent democratic state.

Since then Riga has made huge efforts to establish itself not only as a vibrant capital of Latvia but also as the major city in the Baltics. Although in terms of size it is the largest of the Baltic capitals, in terms of influence it faces tough competition from the other Baltic capitals. Even within Latvia, its trading status is frequently under threat from the port of Ventspils. Major strides have however been made in improving the city. Many buildings have been restored or rebuilt (most notably the Blackheads' House), infrastructure has been improved and the economy expanded. Since its accession to NATO and the European Union in 2004, the city looks forward to consolidating this progress and establishing itself as a major European capital.

Dates in the history of Riga

1201   Official date of the foundation of Riga by Bishop Albert of Bremen. German domination continues for almost 400 years
1211   Foundations of the Dome Cathedral in Riga are laid
1282   Riga joins the Hanseatic League
1521   The Reformation arrives in Riga
1561   Riga falls to the Polish/Lithuanian Empire
1601   Riga falls to Gustavus Adolphus II of Sweden
1681   Riga's first newspaper, the *Rigische Nouvellen*, is established
1701   First pontoon bridge is built across the River Daugava in Riga

1710	Riga surrenders to the Russians, who win the Northern War against Sweden
1767	Population of Riga stands at 16,300
1812	Riga's suburbs are set on fire to deflect a Napoleonic invasion
1817	Serfs are emancipated, 40 years earlier than in Russia
1820s	Throughout the century Latvian nationalism increases
1861	Railway comes to Riga
1873	Folk-song festival is established in Riga
1887	Electricity generation station is built in Riga
1896	Art nouveau buildings are erected in Riga from around 1896 to 1913
1897	Population of Riga rises to 255,879
1904	A Scot, George Armisted, is mayor of Riga 1904–12
1905	Suppression of a workers' demonstration in Riga, killing 70 people
1916	First Latvian mayor of Riga is elected
1917	Riga surrenders to the Germans
1918	Latvian independence is proclaimed on November 18 in the National Theatre
1935	Freedom Monument is erected in the centre of Riga
1939	Soviet Union establishes a military presence in Riga
1940	Thousands of citizens begin to be deported to Siberia and central Asia
1941	Nazis arrive to 'liberate' Riga from the USSR. The Riga ghetto is set up.
1944	Soviet Army arrives to 'liberate' Riga from the Nazis

History

1949	Massive deportations to Siberia
1988	First demonstrations in Riga against the Soviet occupation
1990	Population of Riga stands at 910,000
1991	Latvian independence is achieved
1993	The lat replaces the rouble as the national currency
2001	Riga celebrates 800 years since its foundation
2003	Riga hosts the Eurovision Song Contest
2004	Latvia joins NATO and the European Union

POLITICS

Since independence the country has had a succession of prime ministers and governments, including several coalitions. A new government came into office in March 2004. It is a centre-right coalition led by Indulis Emsis of the Union of Greens and Farmers (ZZS), but even with the support of two other parties, it holds only 46 of the 100 seats in the Saeima, Latvia's parliament, and seems unlikely to be able to maintain dominance for long. In 1999 the Saeima elected its first female president, Vaira Vīķe-Freiberga, a Canadian Latvian. Since then she has been re-elected and is expected to serve until 2007.

Riga has its own City Council with 60 deputies and its own mayor, since 2001 Gundars Bojars, a former deputy chairman of the Saeima. Currently the mayor is elected by the Saeima but there is discussion as to whether future mayors should be directly elected by the citizens of Riga.

Contexts

ECONOMY

Latvia introduced its own currency, the lat, to replace the rouble in 1993. Two years later the country suffered a major banking crisis when the largest bank, Banka Baltija, was declared insolvent. Better banking standards, however, gradually led to a more stable situation and, after weathering the Russian economic crisis, the economy is currently stable and growing. Incomes remain low, however, and when Latvia entered the European Union in mid-2004 it had the lowest gross domestic product per capita of all the new EU accession states, although one which was growing quickly. GDP growth has been boosted by buoyant private consumption and a credit boom. The industrial sector has also performed well, as Latvia's products have found new markets outside the Baltic states and have regained some market share in Russia. Unemployment is lower in Riga than in many other parts of Latvia.

PEOPLE

The population of Riga currently stands at 739,232, down from its peak of over 900,000 at the end of the period of Soviet occupation, due partly to the Soviet withdrawal but also to the low birth rate throughout the country. Latvians are not in the majority in Riga: only 42% of the population is Latvian, compared with 43% who are Russian and 15% from other ethnic groups, whereas in the country as a whole Latvians make up 58% of the population and Russians 30%.

As Latvia has tried to extricate itself from many of its former links with the USSR there have been continuing problems regarding the status of former Soviet

People

citizens, many of whom have been disenfranchised by residence and language qualifications deliberately drafted to exclude citizens of the former colonial power from voting on Latvia's future. In 1998 a referendum granted citizenship to children born in Latvia to non-citizens after 1991; others need to pass a language qualification. Although knowledge of the Latvian language has increased in recent years (the 2000 census revealed that 79% of the population now know Latvian), a considerable number of long-term Latvian residents do not know the language. Some 21% of the adult population are currently non-citizens and, unlike in the other Baltic states, these people are not allowed to vote in elections.

Ethnic Latvians are often said to be reserved, sometimes even cold. Most people who stay more than a short time in Riga, however, find that once the ice is broken, friendships are warm and long lasting. Locals often say too that the Latvian character, like the country itself, lies midway between the Estonians and the Lithuanians. According to this theory, the Latvian character is less emotional that the Lithuanians but more flamboyant than the notoriously unemotional Estonians.

RELIGION

Since the Reformation Latvia has been primarily a Lutheran country, and even today there are far more Lutheran than Catholic or Russian Orthodox believers. During the Soviet occupation many churches were turned into sports halls or other entertainment areas, and others were pulled down or left to deteriorate. Since independence however many churches have been restored. Riga has a large number of churches of most faiths, including a church for Old Believers and a synagogue, as well as churches for most mainstream Christian groups (see page 42 for a list of places and times of worship).

Before the arrival of Christianity Latvians were animists: they believed in the divinity of all living things, from people to animals, birds and trees. Although these beliefs have long since disappeared, there remain references to spirits in folk songs and stories, and Jāņi, the midsummer holiday which is enthusiastically celebrated in Riga and throughout Latvia, is connected with early pagan traditions.

BUSINESS

Latvians are generally easy to do business with: they have a direct, no-nonsense approach and want to achieve things quickly and efficiently. They frequently entertain over lunch but do not expect or generally offer lavish evening entertainment. English is now firmly established as the language of business and is spoken by everyone seriously interested in working with people from outside Latvia. You will find branches of the major accountants and consultants in Riga, as well as English-speaking lawyers and highly qualified translators. All the major hotels have business centres and there is no shortage of the usual photocopying and equipment hire companies throughout central Riga.

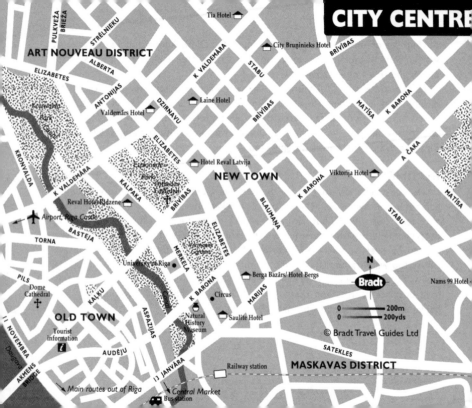

Planning

THE CITY – A PRACTICAL OVERVIEW

Riga is an ideal weekend break destination. Only two and a half hours' flight from London, a Friday evening flight will give you two full days in the city before catching a flight back home on Monday. This is not to say that a longer stay is not worthwhile. It is – and two days will probably make you leave wanting to come back and see more.

Even in two days, however, you will quickly get a feel for the city. The layout is easy: there is an Old Town and a New Town, separated by parks and a canal. To the west of the Old Town is the majestic River Daugava, flowing north into the Gulf of Riga, around 10km away after winding its way from the Russian border through the whole of rural Latvia. For a quick (and literal) overview of the city, go up the tower of St Peter's Church in the Old Town or to the skyline bar of the Reval Hotel Latvija in the New Town and see the city at your feet.

Whether you stay in the Old Town or the New Town (and New isn't very new – most of the buildings were erected at the end of the 19th and the beginning of the 20th century), you will be able to walk to most of the places you want to visit. For the Ethnographical Museum or other locations on the outskirts of Riga, buses and trams are frequent and easy to use. Taxis too are abundant and reasonably priced.

St Peter's tower

Riga has become very much a Western capital and whatever you want to buy, from food and drink to English-language books, you are likely to find seven days a week and even 24 hours a day. Daily items tend to be noticeably cheaper than at home, although this is not the place to shop for imported luxury brands.

If you are spending a long weekend here, think about the best time to visit any museums you particularly want to see: most close on Mondays. Most churches (though not the Dome Cathedral) are, however, open every day.

The huge increase in hotels and restaurants in recent years means there is now a wide choice, and visitors should have no problem finding something to suit them. It is possible to sleep and eat cheaply if you search around, but be warned that up-market hotels and restaurants tend to be similarly priced to their equivalents in the UK or the USA.

WHEN TO VISIT

May to September is probably the best time to visit Latvia. The winter months (November to March) can be very cold and wet, although the city can look very beautiful in the snow; summer is warm, even hot, but can also be rainy, especially in July and August; spring and autumn are temperate. The average annual temperature in Riga is 6.6°C, but it can rise to 30°C in summer and go as low as minus 23–25°C in December.

Average monthly temperatures (°C) are as follows:

January	−3.0	July	18.1
February	−0.6	August	18.2
March	−0.4	September	11.2
April	2.7	October	4.5
May	9.0	November	1.4
June	15.5	December	−4.5

What Riga offers varies quite considerably according to the season. The cold winters make indoor events the norm from October to April, while over the summer months more outdoor activities, from open-air concerts and festivals to beer gardens, are on offer, although there generally has to be some provision for rain even in July and August. The opera house and theatres mostly close in July and August, as Latvians head for the coast or the lakes to enjoy the long summer evenings.

Riga is hosting a growing number of festival and events, although relatively few are yet established as regular annual events. If you have particular interests, you should check some of the latest calendars of events (see *Chapter 13* for websites) for the year of your visit. Established summer events include:

June   June 23/24: midsummer celebrations
Riga Opera Festival
Rhythmic Musical Festival in Riga

When to visit

July Sigulda Opera Festival
Cēsis Beer Festival
Riga Summer Singing Festival

August Sacred Music Festival in Riga

SUGGESTED ITINERARIES
One day
- Walk through the Old Town (see Old Town Walks one and two, page 111)
- Have a coffee at one of Riga's new coffee houses
- Try a traditional Latvian lunch
- Spend the afternoon in the art nouveau district (page 124)
- Have a cocktail on the 26th floor of the Reval Hotel Latvija (page 59)
- Have dinner in a restaurant in the Old Town
- Visit the opera or a concert

Two days
In addition to the above:
- Take your time over visiting the Old Town, incorporating visits to museums
- Visit the State Museum of Art (page 146) and the Russian Orthodox Cathedral (page 169)
- Take an afternoon trip to the Open Air Ethnographical Museum (page 159)

- Visit some of the art galleries and antiques shops in the Old and New Towns
- Treat yourself to handmade chocolates
- Choose from a wide variety of evening entertainments

Three days

In addition to the above:
- Take a trip outside Riga, either to Jūrmala on the coast or to Rundāle Palace (page 205)
- Wander through the parks and gardens in central Riga
- Visit the Central Market (page 135) and stock up on local produce
- Take a final look at the city by night

TOURIST INFORMATION

If you need detailed information, suggestions for particular trips or other specialist information, the staff at the tourist office will be pleased to help. The tourist office can also arrange guides. It is located in the Old Town in the Blackheads' House at 7 Rātslaukums (tel: 704 4377; fax: 704 4378; email: tourinfo@rcc.lv; www.rigatourism.com). Open 10.00–18.00.

Riga is also exceptionally well provided with regularly updated and free city guides, which will answer many of your queries. See page 38 for details.

TOUR OPERATORS

The following specialise in the Baltic states (among other destinations) or in weekend city breaks.

UK

Baltic Holidays 40 Princess St, Manchester M1 6DE; tel: 0870 757 9233; fax: 0870 120 2973; email: info@balticholidays.com; www.balticholidays.com. Two to five day trips to Riga at a variety of hotels; homestays also offered.

Bridge Travel Bridge House, 55–59 High Rd, Broxbourne, Herts EN10 7DT; tel: 0870 191 7271; fax: 01992 456609; email: cities@bridgetravel.co.uk; www.bridgetravel.co.uk. Weekend breaks to Riga.

Martin Randall Travel Voysey House, Barley Mow Passage, London W4 4PH; tel: 020 8742 3355; email: info@martinrandall.co.uk; www.martinrandall.com. Specialise in art, music and architecture, including trips to the Riga Opera Festival.

Operas Abroad The Tower, Mill Lane, Rainhill, Prescot, Merseyside L35 6NE; tel/fax: 0151 493 0382; email: info@operasabroad.com; www.operasabroad.com

Regent Holidays (UK) Ltd 15 John St, Bristol BS1 2HR, tel: 0117 921 1711; fax: 0117 925 4866; email: regent@regent-holidays.co.uk; www.regent-holidays.co.uk. Organise weekend and longer trips to Riga and other destinations in Latvia and all the Baltic states.

Scantours 47 Whitcomb St, London WC2H 7DH; tel: 020 7839 2927; fax: 020 7839 5891; email: info@scantours.com; www.scantours.co.uk. Offer three- and six-day city breaks in Riga.

Specialised Tours 4 Copthorne Bank, Copthorne, Crawley, West Sussex RH10 3QX; tel: 01342 712785; fax: 01342 717042; email: info@specialisedtours.com; www.specialisedtours.com. Weekend breaks to Riga.

Traveleditions 69–85 Tabernacle St, London EC2A 4BD; tel: 020 7251 0045; fax: 020 7251 7399; email: tours@traveleditions.co.uk; www.traveleditions.co.uk. Weekend breaks to Riga.

US

Amest Travel 16 Ocean Parkway #19, New York 11218; tel: 718 360 0886; fax: 718 851 4175; email: info@amest.com; www.amest.com

Value World Tours Plaza del Lago Building, Suite 203, 17220 Newhope St, Fountain Valley, CA 92708; tel: 714 556 8258; fax: 714 556 6125; email: travel@vwtours.com; www.vwtours.com

Vytis Tours 40–24 235th St, Douglaston, New York 11363; tel: 800 778 9847 or 718 423 6161; fax: 718 423 3979; email: tours@vytistours.com; www.vytistours.com

Canada

Valhalla Travel and Tours 120 Newkirk Rd, Unit 25, Richmond Hill, Ontario 4C 9S7; tel: 800 265 0459 or 905 737 1300; email: info@valhallatravel.com; www.valhallatravel.com

RED TAPE
Passports and visas

You will need a valid full passport. No visa is needed for EU, US, Canadian, Australian, New Zealand or Japanese citizens visiting Latvia. Citizens of these countries may stay up to 90 days within a period of six months to one year, depending on nationality. If you want to stay in Latvia for more than 90 days you will need a residency permit or special visa. Persons who need a visa may obtain one for ten days or 30 days, and it can be extended for a maximum of 90 days in total in any one year. The cost of a visa can vary depending on your country of origin, as can the time it will take you to get one. You are advised to seek advice from your nearest Latvian embassy (see below).

Obtaining a residence permit can be a lengthy process, and may entail a wait of up to three months. The application must be made before your visa expires. For further and up-to-date information contact your nearest Latvian embassy or the Foreigners' Service Centre of the Citizenship and Migration Board in Riga, at 1 Alunāna, Riga (tel: 721 96 56; email: aad@pmlp.gov.lv; www.pmlp.gov.lv).

Latvian embassies

Australia (Consulate) 8 Barr-Smith St, Tusmore, SA 5064; tel: 8833 33 123; fax: 8833 33 227; email: fsvilans@ozemail.com.au

Canada 280 Albert St, Suite 300, Ottawa, Ontario L4C 9S7; tel: 613 238 6014; fax: 613 238 7044; email: consulate.canada@mfa.gov.lv

Denmark Rosbaeksvej 17, DK-2100 Copenhagen, tel: 39 27 60 00; email: embassy.denmark@mfa.gov.lv

Estonia 10 Tõnismägi Str, 10119 Tallinn; tel: 627 7850; fax: 627 7855; email: embassy.estonia@mfa.gov.lv

France 6 Villa Said, Paris 16; tel: 01 53 64 58 10; fax: 01 53 64 58 19; email: embassy.france@mfa.gov.lv
Germany Reinerzstrasse 40/41, 14193 Berlin; tel: 49 308 260 0222; fax: 49 308 260 0233; email: embassy.germany@mfa.gov.lv
Ireland 14 Lower Leeson St, Dublin 2; tel: 1 662 1610; fax: 1 662 1599; email: embassy.ireland@mfa.gov.lv
Lithuania 76 M K Čiurlionio Str, 2009 Vilnius; tel: 5213 1260; fax: 5213 1130; email: embassy.lithuania@mfa.gov.lv
South Africa (Consul) 4 Lafayette, 39 Harrow Rd, Sandhurst, Sandton 2916; tel: 11 783 9442; fax: 11 783 9450; email: neishlos@icon.co.za
United Kingdom 45 Nottingham Pl, London W1U 5LY; tel: 020 7312 0040; fax: 020 7312 0042; email: embassy.uk@mfa.gov.lv
USA 4325 17th Street NW, Washington DC 20011; tel: 202 726 8213; fax: 202 726 6785; email: embassy.usa@mfa.gov.lv

Customs

It is forbidden to import arms, explosives, drugs or pornography. On leaving Latvia, you should declare any large quantities of jewellery or other valuables you are taking out of the country. If you export any item made in Latvia and over 50 years old it may be subject to duty at 20% of its value. There are no restrictions on bringing in or taking out currency. For up-to-date information you should contact your local embassy, and for enquiries on works of art, the

Red tape

Ministry of Culture, 22 Pils iela (1st floor), Riga (tel: 721 4100; fax: 722 7916); the relevant department is open on weekdays 08.30–17.00.

GETTING THERE AND AWAY

The majority of visitors from countries in Europe or from the Americas are likely to travel by air.

By air

From the UK, British Airways and Air Baltic both operate direct flights from London Heathrow to Riga. Air Baltic flies daily except Saturdays and BA every day except Monday and Wednesday. The flight takes about two and a half hours. In August 2004 Air Baltic started direct flights from Manchester to Riga. Ryanair now also operates a daily service from Stansted to Riga. The flight leaves Stansted at 14.40 and arrives in Riga at 19.15, but the return flight is less convenient, leaving Riga at 22.50 and arriving at Stansted at 23.25. There are also regular flights to Riga from Amsterdam, Berlin, Brussels, Copenhagen, Dublin, Frankfurt, Hamburg, Helsinki, Kiev, Milan, Minsk, Moscow, Munich, Oslo, Prague, Stockholm, Tallinn, Vienna, Vilnius and Warsaw.

Fares fluctuate frequently and for short-break visitors it is often cheaper to book a package than flights and hotels separately. The lowest fares are usually available in winter, spring and autumn, but invariably increase over Christmas and Easter. To secure reasonable prices in the summer, it is important to book well in advance. While Riga has not yet become as popular a weekend destination as

Tallinn in Estonia, with the entry of Latvia into the EU in 2004 it is likely that more low-cost carriers may start services from the UK and elsewhere in Europe.

For travellers from the USA, SAS and Finnair offer good connections via Copenhagen and Stockholm, but given the very low fares usually available to London from the USA and Canada, it may often be cheaper to break the journey in London and take a separate package from there. Via London is always the best route for tourists from Australia and New Zealand, as well as from South Africa.

Airline addresses/telephone numbers in Riga are as follows:

Aeroflot Airport; tel: 720 7472; city centre: 6 Ģertrūdes iela, tel: 727 8774

Air Baltic Airport; tel: 720 7777, email: reservations@airbaltic.lv; www.airbaltic.lv; city centre: 15 Kaļķu iela; tel: 722 9166

British Airways Airport; tel: 720 7097; www.britishairways.com; city centre: 4/111a Torņa iela; tel: 732 6737

CSA Airport; tel: 720 7636; email: csa-riga@apollo.lv; www.czech-airlines.com

Estonia Air 22 Aspāzijas bulvāris (Hotel Riga); tel: 721 4860; email: riga@estonian-air.ee; www.estonian-air.ee

Finnair Airport; tel: 720 7010; www.finnair.lv

KLM Airport; tel: 766 8600; www.klm.com

LOT 5 Mazā Pils iela; tel: 722 7234; email: lotrix@lot.com; www.lot.com

Lufthansa Airport; tel: 750 7711; email: lufthansa@apollo.lv; www.lufthansa.com

SAS 15 Kaļķu iela; tel: 720 7777

Getting there and away

By train

It is less likely that you will choose to travel to Riga by train unless you are using the train to travel from Moscow or St Petersburg. The train journey from Moscow to Riga takes about 12½ hours; from St Petersburg to Riga 12 hours. All trains to Riga arrive in Riga Central Station (*centrālā stacija*) which is a short walk from the Old Town [1 B4]. International trains arrive at platform 2. There are automatic luggage lockers below the Central Hall (*centrālā zāle*). The price is Ls0.50 to Ls1.00 per day; 04.30 to midnight. There are currency exchanges in tunnels A and B and banks to the left and right of the Central Hall, as well as several money withdrawal machines.

By coach

The bus station in Riga is next to the railway station [1 B4]. The left-luggage office is open 05.30 to midnight (Ls0.20/0.40 an hour, and Ls0.10 per extra hour). The bus station is quite close to the Old Town. Follow signs to Vecriga–Vaļņu iela. Tram 7 stops in front of the bus station and is only one stop from the centre. Pay Ls0.20 to the conductor on the bus.

By sea

There are regular ferries from Lithuania and Stockholm to Riga. The ferry terminal is around 1km to the north of the Old Town. There is a money exchange bureau in the terminal (09.00–18.00). To get to the Old Town, take tram number 5, 7 or 9 from Ausekļa iela for two stops.

Planning

By car

If you decide to drive you will have to cope with the border crossings which may still entail a wait of up to one hour. You should take an international driving licence and contact your insurers about any special requirements and any extra premium you will almost certainly have to pay. The standard green card used in most of western Europe is not recognised in Latvia. Seek advice from your local motoring organisation for up-to-date requirements. It is probably wiser to hire a car locally. For details of the major car hire companies operating in Latvia see page 46.

HEALTH

For an emergency ambulance, phone 03.

Hospitals and medical care are of a reasonable standard but not up to Western standards. You are advised to take out health insurance. If you are unlucky enough to contract a major illness while in Riga, it is probably best to fly home. If you do need treatment in Riga, however, there are a number of places where you can be guaranteed help from English-speaking professionals:

ARS Medical practice. 5 Skolas iela; tel: 720 1001 or 720 1003
A&S Health Care Private dental clinic. 60 Lāčplēša iela; tel: 728 9516
Latvian-American Eye Centre 93 Tallinas iela; tel: 727 2257

Standards of hygiene are generally good, but you should avoid drinking tap water: it is advisable to stick to bottled water.

Health

No vaccinations are required for travel to Latvia. If you are camping or staying by the sea, for example in Jūrmala, in May to September there is a small risk of encephalitis from ticks found in the forests. Injections are available, and now can be done within three to four weeks of travelling. Whether you opt for vaccination or not, simple precautions such as using tick repellents and wearing hats and long trousers tucked into boots should suffice.

Pharmacies

Pharmacies are easy to find in Riga. Look for the word *Aptieka* (pharmacy). Many have extended opening hours and several pharmacies are open 24 hours, including:

Kamēlijas Aptieka 74 Brīvības iela; tel: 729 3514
Saules Aptieka 230 Brīvības iela; tel: 755 3368
Tallinas Aptieka 57b Tallinas iela; tel: 731 4211
Vecpilsētas Aptieka 20 Audēju iela; tel: 721 33 40 or 722 38 26

Other pharmacies include:

In the Old Town: **Lauvas Aptieka** (Lion pharmacy), 20 Kaļķu iela; tel: 722 6519
In the New Town: **Mēness Aptieka** 91/93 Elizabetes iela; tel: 750 2230

CRIME AND PERSONAL SAFETY

To call the police in an emergency, dial 02.

Crime has increased in all the Baltic states since they gained their independence, but by and large they are pretty safe places for travellers. Avoid leaving money or valuables in your hotel room, and make sure you carry only modest sums of money on you at any time. Make sure you have a contact number to telephone your credit card company to cancel your account if your card is stolen. Street robbery remains relatively rare, but avoid flaunting large amounts of money or valuables. In particular, be careful when you leave clubs or bars late at night and try not to walk back to your hotel unaccompanied. As in most cities, it is best to avoid parks and streets next to parks after dark. Cars are the most vulnerable objects of crimes: crook locks and other devices are in common use and should be used on hire cars if you leave them for long periods of time. Try to park in guarded and well-lit spots overnight.

The police are well trained and unobtrusive, although they do carry out spot checks on cars. If you do run into trouble with the police remember that the officer must produce his identification, he must tell you why you have been detained (if you have been arrested) and you cannot in any event be held by the police for longer than 72 hours (in the case of a serious offence) or three hours (for a minor, administrative offence). As in most countries, you are entitled to have a lawyer present when the police question you. Contact your embassy or consulate if you need legal help (see page 42 for embassy details).

Women are unlikely to be subject to any dangers in Latvia that they would not experience elsewhere in Europe. It is wise to take the usual precautions on personal safety, especially when travelling alone, but no special measures are needed.

WHAT TO TAKE

Winter can be very cold, so make sure you take enough warm clothes if you are going to Riga between October and May. June, July and August are usually warmer, but even so you will probably need a jacket or similar most of the time. You should also always take something rainproof, even in summer, since the weather is unreliable, and July and August often have heavy rain. Weather forecasting can be difficult in Riga due to the closeness to the sea and the frequently changing wind directions, but it is always worth checking an internet weather service just before you leave. See for example www.wunderground.com/global/stations/26422.html.

ELECTRICITY

The electric current in Latvia, as in most of continental Europe, is 220 volts AC, 50 Hz. Plugs are the standard European two-pin variety so take an adaptor from the UK.

MONEY
Currency

The lat is the official currency of Latvia (in Latvian the singular is *lats*, the plural *lati*). There are 100 santīmi to the *lat* (the singular is *santīms*, the plural *santīmi*). The lat comes in notes in denominations of 5, 10, 20, 50, 100 and 500 lats, and in the form of 1 and 2 lat coins. In November 2004 exchange rates were £1 = Ls0.97, US$1 = Ls0.52, €1 = Ls0.68. For the latest exchange rates, check your daily newspaper or www.xe.com/ucc/full.shtml/.

Budgeting

If you take a package holiday to Riga, you are not likely to need to change much money at all – just enough for drinks and souvenirs and so on. If you are travelling independently, you are advised to change money as you go, changing as little as possible at one time (although there is no problem in changing larger notes back into your domestic currency). Allow about £60–90 (US$115–170) a night for accommodation in a double room in a good hotel in Riga, or £30–50 (US$55–95) for a tourist-class hotel. A good restaurant meal (two courses and wine for two) will cost about £25–35 (US$45–65). An overnight stay in a more modest hotel is likely to cost about £15 (US$28) per person per night. You can eat out in the cheaper restaurants for as little as £3–5 (US$5.50–9.00) per person.

The following prices may give you some idea of the cost of living:

Snickers bar	Ls0.23
Loaf of white bread	Ls0.25
Bottle of vodka (1 litre)	Ls4.50
Bottle of local beer (0.5l)	Ls0.40

Money

20 Marlboro cigarettes	Ls0.75
Cup of coffee	From Ls0.50 for a basic cup to over Ls1 for a latte or cappuccino in a coffee house

Tipping

Tipping is not compulsory but is common. It is usual to acknowledge good service by leaving an extra 10%. In some restaurants menus will indicate whether service is included.

Practicalities

CHANGING MONEY AND CREDIT CARDS
Changing money

You can change money easily; there is a bureau de change at Riga airport, though it offers a poor exchange rate, and you can change money at most banks, hotels and, most conveniently, at exchange booths/shops around Riga. Look for the sign *Valūtas Maiņas*. Note that if you are arriving late in the evening, the bureau de change at the airport may be closed, so it is a good idea to change at least a small amount of money before you leave your home country. You can buy lats in some (but not all) exchange bureaux at London Heathrow (try Travelex).

In Riga itself, you will get a better rate at exchange booths than at the hotels or banks. There are several 24-hour bureaux de change in Riga, including Marika at 14 Basteja bulvāris, 14 Marijas iela and 30 Brīvības iela. Many bureaux stay open until late at night. Exchange bureaux do not accept travellers' cheques and they can be difficult and time-consuming to change in banks; it is better not to bring them.

Try to carry a certain amount of money in small change since museum entrance charges are cheap (usually no more than Ls1), as are most things you are likely to need on a day-to-day basis (drinks, bus fares and so on); large denomination notes are rarely welcome. As prices are low, avoid changing large sums. Street crime is rare in Latvia, and the atmosphere is generally relaxed. However, you should avoid carrying large sums in cash, and it is wise to leave money and valuables in a hotel safe; carry some cash in a money belt.

Credit cards

For major purchases, hotels and restaurants, credit cards are widely accepted, and cash dispensers (which take major credit cards, in particular Mastercard and Visa) are common in Riga.

LOCAL MEDIA

Riga is extremely well provided with up-to-date English-language information for visitors. The *Baltic Times*, published weekly on a Thursday, is the best English-language source of news for all three Baltic republics. It also lists exhibitions and concerts. In addition no fewer than five bi-monthly guides are widely available at no cost. At the airport you can usually pick up the latest *Riga This Week* while you are waiting for your luggage to be delivered. If not, your hotel will certainly provide a copy and/or a copy of *Riga in Your Pocket, Riga Guide, Welcome* or the *City Paper* (which also covers Tallinn and Vilnius). Of these the most informative are *Riga in Your Pocket*, an independent review, and *Riga This Week*. These can be accessed online if you need information prior to your trip to Riga: www.inyourpocket.com and www.rigathisweek.lv.

European editions of British and American newspapers are on sale in Riga at the larger hotels on the day of publication.

Practicalities

Although there are no local radio or television stations that transmit in English, if you have access to FM radio you may be interested in:

96.2 Radio Naba A student station playing all types of non-classical music.

99.5 Russkoje Radio Easy listening Russian channel.

100.5 BBC World Service

103.7 Klassika Classical music.

105.2 Radio SWH Popular Latvian music.

COMMUNICATIONS
Telephones

The country code for Latvia, for calls from outside the country, is 371. To call Riga from abroad therefore dial 371, the city code of 2, and then the seven-digit number.

To make an international call from Latvia, dial 00 followed by the country code.

Australia	61	Ireland	353
Canada	1	Italy	39
Estonia	372	Lithuania	370
Finland	358	UK	44
France	33	USA	1
Germany	49		

To use a public payphone in Riga you normally need a phonecard (Telekarte). These can be bought at kiosks, stores, post offices etc, wherever you see the sign Telekarte, and are available for Ls 2, 3 or 5. Some phones also take coins. The post office at 1 Stacijas laukums and Plus Punkts kiosks also sell Interkarte, an international prepaid calling card that can also be used with mobile phones (tel: 707 3434; www.baltia.net).

To call towns outside Riga from Riga, prefix the city code:

Bauska   39   Cēsis   41

Mobile phones
More Latvians now have mobile phones than land lines. To call mobile phones in Riga, just dial the seven-digit code. Contact your service provider before leaving in order to set up international roaming. If your own mobile phone does not operate in Latvia, it is possible to rent one from many shops in the centre of the town or from the better hotels. For further information on telephoning contact Lattelkom (tel: 800 80 40; www.lattelkom.lv).

Useful telephone numbers

Fire	01	Directory enquiries	118 or 117
Police	02	Tourist information	704 4377
Ambulance	03		

Post
The most convenient post office (Latvijas Pasts) is at 19 Brīvības bulvāris (www.pasts.lv) and is open 07.00–22.00 Monday to Friday, 08.00–20.00 Saturday

Practicalities

and Sunday. It sells phonecards and postcards, and can help with international calls. Other post offices are at Stacijas laukums (Station Square) and 41–43 Elizabetes iela.

Rates for postcards are Ls0.10 within the Baltics, Ls0.20 for Europe and Ls0.30 for North America. For letters (minimum weight) the rates are Ls0.15 within the Baltics, Ls0.30 for Europe and Ls0.40 for North America (correct in mid-2004).

Internet
All major hotels have a business centre offering a full range of services including internet access, but the charges are high. An alternative is internet cafés, of which Riga has a generous sprinkling, including the sample listed below. Most offer internet access for Ls0.45–0.50 per hour.

In the Old Town
Dualnet Café 17 Peldu iela (next to the Ainavas hotel); tel: 781 44 40. Open 24 hours.
Virtual Travel Bureau 20 Kaļķu iela; tel: 722 8228; email: café@iec.lv. Open 09.30–00.30.

In the New Town
C&I Internet Club 11-308 Merķeļa iela; tel: 721 2040; email: club@icc-info.lv. Open Mon–Fri 8.00–20.00, Sat 09.00–17.00, closed Sun.
Elizabete 75 Elizabetes iela; tel: 728 2876. Open Mon–Fri 09.30–22.00, Sat & Sun 10.00–21.00.

WiFi

The number of wireless hotspots in Riga is growing all the time. If your laptop is equipped with a Wireless LAN card, you should be able to go on-line at:

Hotels OK, Radi un Draugi, Park Hotel, Reval Latvija, Radisson SAS, Riga, Maritim, Gutenbergs, Bruņinieks.

Cafés/restaurants Coffee Nation, Double Café, Melnais Kaķis, Sarkans, Lido Recreational Centre.

EMBASSIES IN RIGA

Canada 20/22 Baznīcas ieal; tel: 781 3945; fax: 781 3960; email: Riga@dfait-maei.qc.ca
Estonia 13 Skolas iela; tel: 781 2020; fax: 781 2029; email: embassy.riga@mfa.ee
Finland 1 Kalpaka bulvāris; tel: 707 8817; fax: 707 8814; email: rii.sanomat@formin.fi
Ireland (Consul) 54 Brīvības iela; tel: 702 5259; fax: 702 5223
Lithuania 24 Rūpniecības iela; tel:732 1519; fax: 732 1589
Russia 2 Antonijas iela; tel: 733 2151; fax: 783 0209; email: rusembas@delfi.lv
UK 5 Alunāna iela; tel: 777 4700; fax: 777 4707; email: british.embassy@apollo.lv
USA 7 Raiņa bulvāris; tel: 703 6200; fax: 782 0047; email: pas@usaembassy.lv

WORSHIP

The majority of churches are Lutheran, with Orthodox churches coming in second place. Few offer services in languages other than Latvian or Russian. There is currently no mosque in Riga.

Church of England St Saviour's, 2a Anglikāņu iela (service in English 11.00 Sun)

Lutheran The Dome (Sun 12.00); St John's (Sun 08.00, 09.00. 11.00); and many others

Old Believers Grebenščikova Church, 73 Krasta iela (services in Church Slavonic at 08.00 and 17.00 on Sun)

Orthodox Orthodox Cathedral, 23 Brīvības iela (services in Church Slavonic at 08.00 and 17.00 Mon–Fri, 07.00, 09.30 and 17.00 on Sat, and 08.00, 10.00 and 17.00 on Sun)

Roman Catholic St Jacob's/St James (page 171), 7 Jāņa iela (the Roman Catholic Cathedral – service in English 10.00 Sun); Our Lady of Sorrows, Lielā Pils iela

Synagogue 6–8 Peitavas iela (Hebrew service at 09.30 Sat)

SMOKING

Despite recent government efforts, smoking continues to be popular in Latvia. Smoking is illegal in public buildings but allowed in restaurants and bars. A recent attempt by Jūrmala to ban smoking on its beaches has been declared illegal although the government has said that in future it intends to allow cities and towns to decide for themselves whether to ban smoking or not. As around 33% of the total population and up to 50% of Latvian men smoke (compared with 28% in the UK and 25% of adults in the USA), businesses fear that a ban on smoking could ruin their trade.

TOILETS

Men's toilets are often marked ▼, women's ▲. V (*vīrieši*) or K (*kung*i) are also used for men, and S (*sievietes*) or D (*dāmas*) for women.

Toilets

Local transport

4

AIRPORT TRANSFER

The airport (Lidosta Riga) is about 8km from Riga. A taxi from the airport to the capital should cost a maximum of Ls10. There is also a bus service (the A22 leaves from a bus stop in front of the terminal slightly to the right and on the far side of the airport car park) between the airport and the central bus station. At present it runs every half-hour from 05.50 to 23.15. Buy your ticket (Ls0.20; Ls0.40 for large cases) from the information booth in the terminal building or on board. The journey from the airport to the centre of Riga should take no more than about 20 minutes by taxi, and about 30 minutes by bus.

DRIVING IN RIGA

It is best to see Riga on foot. The Old Town is a relatively small area and most places you are likely to want to visit in the New Town are also most easily reached on foot. A car is therefore not much use for short stays in the city. Note too that access to the Old Town is restricted for cars. To enter the Old Town you need a special pass which costs Ls5 per hour, plus a Ls5 deposit. You can buy the pass at Statoil (1c Eksporta iela) or at Marika Exchange (14 Basteja bulvāris). Note too that on-street parking in the New Town can be hard to find. There are some multi-storey/ underground car parks, including 50 K Valdemāra iela (entrance opposite Antonijas iela) and the Ģertrūdes Centrs near St Gertrude's Church.

If you do drive, be aware that the maximum speed in Riga is 50km/h, seat belts are compulsory, you must always drive with headlights on, various on-the-spot fines are imposed for traffic violations, and that road markings, traffic signs and other drivers' behaviour are not always of the same standard you would expect at home.

CAR HIRE

For visiting areas outside Riga a car is useful, although public transport and organised tours are usually available. Car hire is relatively easy to organise but is quite expensive, as it is in the other Baltic states.

Avis 3 Krasta iela; tel: 722 5876; fax: 782 0441; email: avis@avis.lv; www.avis.lv, and at Riga airport; tel: 720 7353

Baltic Car Lease – Sixt franchisee 28 Kaļķu iela (Hotel de Rome); tel: 722 4022; and at Riga airport; tel: 720 7121; fax: 720 7131; email: car.rent@carlease.lv, www.e-sixt.lv

Budget Rent A Car Airport; tel: 720 7327; fax: 720 7627; email: budget@delfi.lv; www.budget.lv

Easyrent 52 Daugavpils iela; tel: 919 3198; email: office@easyrent.lv; www.easyrent.lv

Europcar 10 Basteja bulvāris; tel: 721 2652; fax: 782 0360; email: www.europcar.lv, and at Riga airport; tel: 720 7825

Hertz 24 Aspāzijas bulvāris; tel: 722 4223, and at Riga airport; tel: 720 7980; fax: 720 7981; www.hertz.lv

National Car Rental Airport; tel: 720 7710

PUBLIC TRANSPORT
Buses and trams

Riga has a well-developed transport system of eight tram lines, 24 trolley bus lines and 39 bus lines. The fare is charged at a flat rate of 20 santīmi (Ls0.20) a journey. Different tickets are needed for each mode of transport and can only be bought on board from the *konduktors*. In addition to the bus, tram and trolleybus, there is another form of transport, the *taksobuss* or *mikroautobuss*, which covers longer distances and costs more, depending on the length of the journey.

The maps in *Riga in Your Pocket* and the yellow Jāņa Sēta Riga map contain information showing public transport routes. There are no route maps at bus/tram stops or inside the buses and trams, but the driver normally announces the name of the approaching stop and other passengers are generally helpful if you ask for directions. (See also the tram map on page 4 on the colour section of this guide.)

The bus station (*autoosta*) is in Prāgas iela [1 B4], close to the main market and on the other side of the railway station (under the bridge) away from the city centre. You can telephone for information (tel: 900 0009), but may find it advisable to attend in person: timetables are on display;x otherwise apply to window 1 for information. Some ticket sellers also speak English.

Trains

Riga has a brand-new, sparkling railway station (Stacijas laukums; tel: 583 2134 for information, or 583 3397 for advance booking [1 B4]), although the same cannot be said of the local trains. Tickets can be bought in the main ticket hall from counters 1 to 13. Most staff selling tickets speak English. The timetables show the track (*ceļš*) the train leaves from. When you go to your train, you will also see the word *perons* (platform) with a number. Ignore this and look for the right track.

The Riga Card

The Riga Card provides access without further charge to trams, buses and trains in Riga and Jūrmala, as well as entitling the holder to free admission or a discount at certain museums. The card costs Ls8 for 24 hours, Ls12 for 48 hours and Ls16 for 72 hours (half price for children under 16). It can be purchased from most hotels, the airport (arrivals hall) and the tourist information office. Although it is convenient, most tourists do not spend this amount of money per day if they pay for individual journeys and tickets as they go.

TAXIS

Taxis are plentiful. You can flag them down anywhere in Riga but in the Old Town there are normally several waiting at both ends of Kaļķu iela, just near the Hotel de Rome [3 D6] and just beyond the Riflemen's Monument [3 A6]. Licensed cabs (these all have yellow licence plates) are fairly reliable provided you check that the meter is on. Rates are 30 santīmi per kilometre during the day, rising to 40 santīmi per kilometre between 22.00 and 6.00. If you want to save money, avoid using taxis waiting outside hotels, as these tend to charge above average rates. To book a taxi, use one of the following free 24-hour numbers: Bona Taxi 800 5050; Riga Taxi 800 1010; Rigas Taksometru parks 800 1313.

TOUR BUSES

A number of firms offer city tours by coach. It is probably best to organise these through your hotel if you are staying in one that offers this facility. Otherwise you can contact one of the agencies below:

Latvia Tours 8 Kaļķu iela; tel: 708 5057, and 13 Marijas iela; tel: 724 3391. Does city tours from 10.00 to 13.00 on Mon and Sat from May to Sep, and also offers regular trips to the Open Air Museum (see page 159) and Motor Museum (see page 156), Rundāle (see page 205) and Sigulda. Trips to Cēsis, Jūrmala and Liepāja can also be arranged.

Patricia LTD 22 Elizabetes iela; tel: 728 4868; email: tour@balticguide.net. Various tours for groups – minibus tours, walking tours, Jewish Riga tours etc. Also offers trips to Sigulda.

Riga Sightseeing Amber Way; tel: 703 7900; email: amberway@inbox.lv. Daily departures from the Latvian Riflemen's Monument and individual sightseeing around Latvia and the Baltic states. Walking tours as well as tours by bus.

BOATS

In summer you can take boat trips on the Daugava departing from 11. Novembra krastmala, close to Akmens bridge. Departures are at 11.00, 13.00, 15.00, 17.00 and 19.00. The trip to Mežaparks and back takes about two hours and costs Ls1. Tel: 953 9184.

CYCLING

Sharing Riga's roads with their notoriously aggressive car drivers is only an activity for the brave, although a growing number of people seem to be cycling in areas away from the city centre. If you do want to hire a bike or a scooter you can do so from:

Gandrs 28 Kalnciema iela; tel: 761 4775; email: gandrs@gandrslv; www.gandrs.lv (in Pārdaugava; cross the Vanšu bridge on foot or take bus number 22). Bikes costs Ls1 per hour or Ls5 for the day, plus a deposit of Ls20.

Suzuki 51 Tallinas iela; tel: 731 2926; email: ekstrom@ekstrom.lv; www.ekstrom.lv. Scooter hire from Ls12–15 per day, plus a deposit of Ls50–100, depending on the scooter.

Accommodation

5

Riga offers a wide choice of accommodation. If money is no object, you can choose from an ever-growing number of luxury hotels, many conveniently situated in the Old Town. For budget travellers there are some very acceptable options too: some of these are located away from the centre but most are on tram routes, which makes getting into the Old Town an easy and relatively quick matter. During 2005, many hotels were being built in all categories and in different parts of the town which should reduce prices in 2006. It is advisable to book well ahead if you want a room in a particular price range or location, especially in summer. Otherwise, although you will always find somewhere to stay, it may not be exactly what you want.

An alternative to staying in Riga, particularly in summer, is to book a hotel in nearby Jūrmala, Riga's seaside resort. Jūrmala is about 20 minutes from Riga by car and about 40 minutes by train (see page 193). Jūrmala has some attractive and recently restored small hotels, as well as larger hotels with views over the Gulf of Riga. However, if you have only a few days in Riga, you probably won't want to travel backwards and forwards every day.

There is currently no tourist information service at the airport, although there are plenty of telephones if you want to find a hotel yourself before going into town. Prices of Riga hotels are often quoted in US dollars and/or euros on websites and brochures but you will always need to make payment in lats. The rates quoted by hotels generally include a buffet breakfast and VAT, unless otherwise specified.

All the quality hotels take credit cards. In practice, there tends to be little difference between prices for single rooms and prices for doubles, and single travellers will often be given a double room anyway.

If you book directly, a double room in a luxury hotel will cost from £90/US$170 upwards, from £60/US$115 in a first-class hotel, and from around £30/US$55 in a tourist-class hotel. Rooms in budget hotels can be found for £12/US$22 upwards, while dormitory beds in hostels can be found from £4/US$7 per person. Note that the prices quoted for superior hotels are maximum rates. If you book your holiday through a tour operator you will benefit from lower package rates. Discounts are also offered by some chains if you book hotels in Riga and Vilnius or Tallinn at the same time. As ever, it is always worth checking internet booking agencies for special offers.

LUXURY HOTELS

Hotel Bergs In the Berga Bazārs, 83/85 Elizabetes iela; tel. 777 0900; fax: 777 0940; email: reservation@hotelbergs.lv, www.hotelbergs.lv [1 C3]
One of Riga's most recently opened hotels, the Hotel Bergs is in the Berga Bazārs shopping area on the edge of the New Town. The hotel and surrounding area is named after the Bergs family who lived in Riga before World War II and whose descendants now run the hotel. The monumental exterior is in contrast to the subtler interior décor. Most of the 38 apartments have kitchenettes; all are spacious and tastefully decorated. The hotel is suitable for tourists, many of whom will also enjoy the handmade chocolates and other exclusive products on sale in the adjoining shopping area, but it also has some of Riga's most

comprehensive business facilities, as well as an elegant and acclaimed restaurant. Prices for suites range from Ls89 to Ls199. Lower rates may be available at the weekend.

Grand Palace Hotel 12 Pils iela; tel: 704 4000; fax: 704 4001; email: grandpalace@schlossle-hotels.com; www.schlossle-hotels.com [2 B3]
Superbly located near the Dome Cathedral, this luxury hotel opened in 2001 and is probably the most expensive in the Old Town, with rooms at Ls130–172 and suites at Ls263–367. Although the building is old, the hotel has all modern facilities, including a fitness centre, sauna and steam room. Each room has a gold, white and blue decorative scheme and antique-style furniture but also satellite TV and internet access. There are two restaurants, the light and airy Orangerie and the velvet-curtained Seasons.

Hotel de Rome 28 Kaļķu iela; tel. 708 7600; fax: 708 7606; email: reservation@derome.lv; www.derome.lv [3 D6]
At the edge of the Old Town, this German-run 4-star hotel is one of the best in Riga. The location, overlooking the Freedom Monument and surrounding parks – of which there is a terrific view from the restaurant – on the edge of the Old Town but within easy reach of the New, is ideal for the tourist. But it is also within easy reach of all the government offices, ministries and many company headquarters, so is suitable for anyone visiting Riga on business. The standard of accommodation and of the common parts is high. The German Otto Schwarz restaurant offers an excellent breakfast and first-class meals at other times of day. It has 90 rooms (10 single, 60 doubles and 20 luxury suites). Prices start from about Ls91 for a single room, and Ls100 for a double, including breakfast.

Luxury hotels

Park OK Hotel 43 Mazā Nometņu iela; tel: 789 4860; fax: 789 2702; email: parkhotel@okhotel.lv; www.okhotel.lv [off 3 B7]
Not to be confused with the OK Hotel (see page 63), this is a super-luxurious and super-expensive hotel on the far side of the River Daugava, set in parkland around 4km from the town centre. Suites start at Ls270 and go up to Ls650 for the presidential suite. Included in the lower prices is a welcome drink, half/full board, a butler, a trip to Jūrmala in the summer and an Old Riga tour.

Reval Hotel Ridzene 1 Reimersa iela; tel: 732 4433; fax: 732 2600; email: ridzene@revalhotels.com; www.revalhotels.com [1 A3]
Formerly a Soviet hotel, the Ridzene has been elegantly refurbished and is now part of the Reval group. It is located at the side of the Esplanade Park in the New Town, close to many embassies and international businesses, whose visitors are among the hotel's main clients. From the sauna you can enjoy superb views over the New Town. The Piramida restaurant in the glass pyramid is amongst the best in Riga. Room prices range from Ls112 for a single room to Ls123 for a double.

Radisson SAS Daugava Hotel 24 Kuģu iela; tel: 706 1111; fax: 706 1100; email: info.riga@radissonsas.com; www.radissonsas.com [off 3 B7]
This is one of the leading business hotels in the Baltics. It is an international-standard business hotel with 361 rooms and suites, including 2 floors of 'business class' rooms which have their own lounge for drinks and are fully equipped for business needs, including 2 telephone lines for internet access. There is security parking, 24-hour room service and

cable TV. With 10 air-conditioned conference rooms the hotel can lay on conferences for up to 360 delegates. A business service offers translation, secretarial and other commercial services. The Grill Room restaurant is highly recommended. There is a modern fitness centre, sauna, swimming pool and shops. The Radisson, however, is very much a business hotel. It is a rather unimaginative white block of a building and is on 'the wrong side' of the Daugava away from the main part of the city, but is quiet and has good views over the river. It offers free transfers from the airport and an hourly shuttle bus to the Old Town. Prices are from Ls76 for a single room to L82 for a double.

FIRST-CLASS HOTELS

Ainavas 23 Peldu iela; tel: 781 4316; fax: 781 4317; email: reservations@ainavas.lv; www.ainavas.lv [3 B8]

This hotel, opened in 2001, has only 22 rooms but each has a different colour scheme and décor based on the browns or greens of Latvia's countryside ('*ainavas*' means landscape). The tone is set in the lobby bar, which is decorated with wood and flowers and where a welcoming fire burns in the hearth. Located in a quiet street in the south of the Old Town, the hotel is suitable for both tourists and business people: each room has a TV with email connection and a dataport. Singles Ls60; standard doubles Ls77.

Centra Hotel 1 Audēju iela; tel: 722 6441; fax: 750 3281; email: hotel@centra.lv; www.centra.lv [3 D8]

The hotel opened in 2000 and is wonderfully situated near St Peter's. It is decorated in a minimalist style with furniture and fabrics which all come from Latvia. Although the area

First-class hotels

nearby can be noisy at night, the rooms are well soundproofed. Rooms on the higher floors offer unusual views of the Old Town. The hotel is excellent value, with rooms at prices below those in similar hotels in the same area. A double typically costs around Ls60.

Domina Inn Riga 11 Pulkveža Brieža; tel: 763 1800; fax: 763 1801; email: info@dominahotels.lv; www.dominahotels.com [1 A1]
This is the first of several hotels to open in 2005 near Albert iela, close to several museums if not quite in the Old Town. With nearly 100 standard rooms, and little sense of design anywhere, it is clearly planned for groups.

Eurolink 22 Aspāzijas bulvāris; tel: 722 0531; fax: 721 6300; email: eurolink@metropole.lv; www.metropole.lv [1 B4]
This is actually the third floor of the Riga Hotel (see page 59) but is run as a separate hotel under joint Latvian–Swedish management. It is conveniently located, opposite the Opera House and within easy reach of the Old and New Towns. When it opened, it was the first 4-star hotel in the capital. Now it offers modern conference and meetings rooms as well as 59 spacious and attractively appointed rooms, a sauna and solarium, and Scandinavian cuisine in the restaurant. Doubles are available from Ls48.

Hotel Gutenbergs 1 Doma laukums; tel: 721 1776; fax: 750 3326; email: hotel@gutenbergs.lv; www.gutenbergs.lv [2 B4]
Located in one of the Baltic states' first publishing houses, hence the name, in a quiet street next to the Dome Cathedral, this hotel has proved very popular since its opening in

2001, and often needs to be booked well in advance. It consists of 2 connected 4-storey buildings, one built in the 17th century and one in the 19th, and has a rich, 19th-century décor throughout. An attraction in summer (which the hotel thinks begins in April) is the rooftop terrace, where you can eat, drink and count the 17 churches visible from this wonderful vantage point. Another speciality is musical lunches in the main restaurant: Latvian musicians play every Sun from 13.00 to 15.00. Prices are from Ls60 for a single and Ls70 for a double room.

Konventenhof or Konventa Sēta 9–11 Kalēju iela; tel: 708 7501–5; fax: 708 7506; email: reservation@konventa.lv; www.konventa.lv [3 D7]
The Konventa Sēta stands out from other hotels in Old Riga in that it is housed on the site of the old city walls in a complex of restored buildings, some dating back to the 13th century. The complex includes a good restaurant, Raibais Balodis, and a bar, Melnais Balodis. Although the hotel's position next to St John's Church could hardly be more central, on occasions it can be noisy at night on the Kalēju iela side. It has 80 rooms and 61 apartments. Single rooms cost Ls46 per night; double rooms and suites from Ls55–70 a night. The hotel also aims at the business market with its 4 conference rooms which can be hired from Ls90–160 a day.

Man-Tess 6 Teātra iela; tel: 721 6056; fax: 782 1249; email: info@mantess.lv; www.mantess.lv [3 D8]
This charming hotel in the centre of Old Riga is an elegant 18th-century house once owned by H Haberland, a Riga architect. It has only 10 rooms (3 doubles, 1 single, 2 suites and 4

offices), each one in a different style (the so-called white room is light and modern, the 18th-century room is furnished in the style of the Hanseatic period). The ground-floor restaurant is exotically decorated (marble, a pond with goldfish, and even caged birds) and is one of the best in the Old Town. Prices range from Ls60 for the single room to Ls100 for a suite. There is a good restaurant, and a banquet/conference hall on the 5th floor.

Maritim Park 1 Slokas iela; tel: 706 9000; fax: 706 9001; email: reservations@maritim.lv; www.maritim.com

A large (240-room) hotel across the river from the Old Town. The location may put off some people, but it is quiet and you can reach the Old Town in about half an hour on foot or by taking the number 2, 4 or 5 trams. On the positive side, the rooms and the Bellevue restaurant on the 11th floor have wonderful views of the Old Town. If walking into town isn't enough exercise, you can use the hotel's gym. Free transport to and from the airport is offered. Standard rooms cost between Ls59–101 for a single, Ls68–110 for a double.

Metropole 36–38 Aspāzijas bulvāris; tel: 722 5411; fax: 721 6140; email: metropole@brovi.lv; www.metropole.lv [1 B4]

Run by the same Latvian–Swedish management team as the Eurolink, the Metropole is suitable for both tourists and business travellers. Built in 1871 the Metropole is the oldest hotel in Riga. It has 80 rooms and has been completely refurbished in an attractive Scandinavian style. It is conveniently located on the edge of the Old Town and only a short walk away from the New Town. Single rooms cost from Ls37, doubles from Ls44 and suites about from Ls75, including breakfast. All rooms are equipped with satellite phone and cable TV.

Accommodation

Nams 99 (House 99) 99 Stabu iela; tel: 731 0762; fax: 731 3204; email: nams-99@delfi.lv; www.nams99.lv [1 E3]

Located in a renovated art nouveau building, the Nams offers 8 apartments and a restaurant. Intended mainly for business users, the rates range from Ls90–150 for an apartment.

Reval Hotel Latvija 55 Elizabetes iela; tel: 777 2222; fax: 777 2221; email: latvija@revalhotels.com; www.revalhotels.com [1 B2]

This was the hotel in which Intourist put up its customers in the days of the USSR, but it has been totally renovated and reopened in May 2001 as a high-quality international-style hotel. It has over 380 rooms, bars and a restaurant. Two advantages are its location in the New Town but just 5 minutes from the Old Town and the views from its upper storeys, its two glass-sided lifts and the skyline bar on the 26th floor. All rooms include satellite TV with games and email possibilities, and minibars with drinks, chocolate and condoms. If you fancy a night in, you can also order a Lulu pizza in your room. Underground parking is available, and on the 27th floor there is a sports and leisure club, equipped with a weight room and sauna. Rooms cost from Ls77 a night for a single and Ls88 for a double.

Riga Hotel 22 Aspāzijas bulvāris; tel: 704 4222; fax: 704 4223; email: info@hotelriga.lv; www.hotelriga.com [1 B4]

On the edge of the Old Town, the Riga is one of the largest and oldest hotels in central Riga. Fully refurbished in 2002/03, all the rooms are pleasantly decorated and spacious. Some have internet dataports. The hotel offers a sauna, bar, conference facilities and a casino. To see what

First-class hotels

the staff got up to before 1991, visit the Occupation Museum which displays the bugging devices they used to monitor phone calls. Singles cost around Ls60 and doubles Ls75.

Rolands 3a Kaļķu iela; tel: 722 0011; fax: 728 1203; email: info@hotelrolands.lv; www.hotelrolands.lv [3 C6]

The hotel was closed in late 2004 due to a legal dispute, but is expected to re-open eventually.

Vecriga 12/14 Gleznotāju iela; tel: 721 6037; fax: 721 45 61; email: vecriga@inet.lv [3 D7]

A small hotel, only 10 double rooms, in a renovated 18th-century house in a quiet street in the Old Town, next to the Palete restaurant. Spacious bedrooms are fitted out with comfortable antique-style furniture, although the bathrooms tend to be small. The hotel has an intimate atmosphere but all modern facilities, and an elegant restaurant. The 10 double rooms cost Ls55–65.

TOURIST-CLASS HOTELS

Albert 33 Dzirnavu; tel: 733 1717; fax: 733 1718; email: info@alberthotel.lv; www.alberthotel.lv [1 A2]

This 11-storey hotel is due to open in September 2005. It will have around 200 rooms, many with good views towards the Old Town.

Avitar 127 Valdemāra iela; tel: 736 4444; fax: 736 4988; email: avitar@apollo.lv; www.avitar.lv [off 1 C1]

A modern hotel a few kilometres away from the centre but on public transport routes. A shuttle service is also available to the airport and to the train and bus stations. Rooms are

Accommodation

clean and spacious, and have cable TV, a telephone and bathroom with shower. A double is Ls36–52.

City Hotel Bruņinieks (The Knight) Bruņinieku iela 6; tel: 731 5140; fax: 731 4310; email: hotel@bruninieks.lv [1 C1]
Originally known just as Bruņinieks, the hotel changed its name to City in 2003 as no foreigner could pronounce the name. A suit of armour is displayed in the foyer, but otherwise this is a perfectly normal 3-star hotel. Some may find the location near the theatre of help and it is sufficiently far from the town centre for the neighbouring shops all to offer Latvian rather than Western prices and for peace and quiet to be assured in the evenings. The lack of a restaurant is a bonus in this respect too. The hotel caters in particular for families, with adjoining rooms available and – for those with smaller children – triple rooms with a roll-up bed. Being just off Brīvības iela, the main road leading to the Freedom Monument, the hotel has a wide range of buses within walking distance. Doubles cost Ls50.

Felicia Hotel 32b Stirnu iela; tel: 759 9942; fax: 754 8145; email: mail@hotelfelicia.com; www.hotelfelicia.com
Take trolley bus number 11 or 18 from the city centre to the Ūnijas iela stop. The hotel is good value for money if you don't mind the 15-minute ride from the town centre. It offers single and double rooms, and also 'minis', very small singles for tourists watching their budget. In addition to a restaurant, 2 bars and a nightclub, it has billiards, saunas, a swimming pool, and even indoor tennis courts. Doubles from Ls30–40; very small singles for around Ls8.

Tourist-class hotels

Forums 45 Vaļņu iela; tel: 781 4680; fax: 781 4682; email: reservation@hotelforums.lv; www.hotelforums.lv [1 B4]

On the edge of the Old Town, near the train station, the hotel has large rooms, with a bath and satellite TV. Despite the modest exterior, it offers elegantly decorated accommodation. Some of the rooms on the upper floors have good views. Breakfast is served, but there is no bar or restaurant, so evenings are quiet. Double rooms cost Ls37–48.

F-Villa 9 Skanstes iela, tel. 751 9922, 751 9921; email: hotel@miests.lv, www.meists.lv

This is a new hotel a few kilometres away from the Old Town. Rooms are comfortable, the environment quiet, green and friendly, and the prices relatively modest. The hotel has a restaurant and bar, and in summer opens a beer terrace. Double rooms cost around Ls24.

Ķeizarmežs Ezermalas iela; tel: 755 7576; fax: 755 7461

Situated on Lake Ķīšezers, near the zoo and Mežaparks, this is a modern complex which may appeal to sports lovers, particularly in summer. There is a well equipped fitness centre, with a swimming pool, squash court, billiards and sauna. Rooms have satellite TV, phone and a private shower or bath. To get there takes around 25 minutes from the Old Town: take trolley bus number 2 to the terminus. Doubles cost from Ls30–38.

Karavella 27 Katrīnas dambis; tel: 732 4597; fax: 783 0187; email: hotel@karavella.lv, www.karavella.lv

With 80 rooms this is a fairly large hotel situated about 10 minutes by car (2km) from the centre of Riga towards the harbour (it is 1km from the marine passenger terminal). You can also reach the hotel on tram number 5 or 9, alighting at Katrīnas iela. Some rooms overlook the harbour; all have cable TV, a refrigerator and telephone. The hotel has a café, which serves snacks and drinks, and a bar. Single rooms from Ls35 and doubles from Ls41.

Laine Hotel 11 Skolas iela; tel: 728 8816 or 728 9823; fax: 728 7658; email: info@laine.lv; www.laine.lv [1 B2]
A small hotel (28 rooms), the Laine has the advantage of being centrally located in the New Town, not far from the Reval Hotel Latvija. With rooms at prices ranging from Ls30–40 for a single room to Ls40–60 for a double room (the cheaper rooms require you to use communal showers) in an elegant art nouveau building, the Laine is exceptionally good value. Most rooms now have satellite TV and a minibar. Do not be put off by the entrance through an unprepossessing courtyard.

Best Western Hotel Mara 186 Kalnciema iela; tel: 770 2718; fax: 770 2708; email: mara@mailbox.riga.lv
Part of the Best Western chain, the Mara has 24 rooms at prices from Ls55 for a single room and Ls65 for a double room. It is out of the centre on the way to the airport, and is the only 3-star hotel near the airport. It operates a shuttle bus to both the airport and the city centre. More of a business hotel than one for tourists. Singles cost Ls45 and doubles Ls50.

OK Hotel 12 Slokas iela; tel: 786 0050; fax: 789 2702; email: service@okhotel.lv; www.okhotel.lv
The OK opened in 2001 and is modest but good value with rooms at Ls45–80. Rooms are adequately furnished and include telephone and cable TV. The disadvantage is its location, over the river from the Old Town. It is a 30-minute walk from the Old Town, but the hotel

Tourist-class hotels

can also be reached quickly by taking tram number 4 or 5 from the Grēcinieku stop to the Kalnciema stop, just over the river. Doubles cost Ls36–55.

Radi un Draugi (Relatives and Friends) 1–3 Mārstaļu iela; tel: 782 0200; fax: 782 0202; email: radi.reservations@draugi.lv; www.draugi.lv [3 D8]
This 76-room hotel right in the centre of the Old Town is comfortable and affordable, as well as being in a superb location. Recently modernised and extended, the hotel has only one drawback: the proximity of 2 pubs means it can get noisy late at night. Singles cost Ls35 and doubles Ls44.

Viktorija 55 A Čaka iela; tel: 701 4111; fax: 701 4140; email: info@hotel-viktorija.lv [1 D2]
This small hotel in a lovely art nouveau building has been partially renovated. The rooms in the renovated area are comfortable and have cable TV. Although not quite central (about 10 minutes by car from the central station and a bit further to the Old Town) it is not too far to walk. Singles are Ls30 and doubles Ls40.

Tia 63 Kr Valdemāra; tel: 733 3918, 733 3035 or 733 3396; fax: 783 0390; email: tia@mail.bkv.lv [1 C1]
A clean and comfortable hotel near the centre with rooms from Ls29 for a single to Ls51 for a suite.

Valdemārs 23 Kr Valdemāra iela; tel: 733 2132 or 733 4462; fax: 733 3001 [1 B2]
Centrally located in an art nouveau building, the Valdemārs is clean and spacious. Room prices range from Ls25 for a single, Ls35 for a double.

BUDGET HOTELS

Baltā Kaza 2 Ēveles iela; tel: 737 8135

The name means 'White Goat'. Located some way out of the centre of Riga, this small and simple hotel looks grim but is clean. Some 35 rooms (it also has dormitories and bunk-bed accommodation) at prices from Ls25 for a double or Ls4 in a dormitory (4 beds to a room). To get there take tram number 3 from Barona iela.

Elias 14 Hamburgas iela; tel: 751 8117

A small hotel with only 7 double rooms near Lake Ķīšezers reached by taking the number 11 tram from Kr Barona iela or the number 9 bus from the station. The location in the Mežaparks is pleasant, and the rooms have private bathrooms and TV. Rooms are Ls16 a night; breakfast not included.

Lidosta at the airport; tel: 720 7149 or 720 7375

A hotel next to the airport (look for the Soviet-style building beyond the car park outside the terminal), and therefore unprepossessing in location as well as appearance. Rooms from Ls9–23; breakfast not included.

Saulīte 12 Merķeļa iela; tel: 722 4546; fax: 722 3629; email: hotel_saulite@one.lv; www.hotel-saulite.lv [1 B4]

Located just opposite the station, the hotel offers basic accommodation at very low prices. Singles Ls8–25; doubles Ls12.

HOSTELS

Riga is not bursting with hostels for backpackers.

Old Town Hostel 50 Kalēju iela; tel: 614 7214; fax: 727 8809; email: oldtown@hostel.lv; www.oldtownhostel.lv

Offers mainly dormitory accommodation, but a few doubles, quads and 2 apartments. Located close to the bus station. Prices include free internet access, washing machines, a kitchen and a common room with TV. Also has baggage storage, a bar and sauna. Dormitory beds Ls10 per person.

Posh Backpackers (Centrāltirgus, Central Market) 5 Pūpolu iela; tel/fax: 721 0917; email: posh@hostel.lv; www.poshbackpackers.lv

Located in one of the old warehouses at the edge of the Central Market, the hostel has spacious single and double rooms, as well as small dormitory rooms. There is no kitchen, only a fridge. Dormitory beds Ls8 per person.

RPRA Hostel 26 Nīcgales 26; tel 754 9012

Clean rooms at cheap prices, but quite a distance from the centre of Riga. The hostel is a member of the International Hostelling Association. To reach the hostel, take trolley bus number 11 or 22 and get off at the Purvciems stop. By taxi the ride from central Riga will cost around Ls3.

Turība 68 Graudu iela; tel: 761 7543; fax: 761 9152; email: viesnica@turiba.lv; www.turiba.lv

With around 250 beds, a kitchen, café, minigolf and internet access, the hostel is part of a business school campus about 20 minutes by public transport from the centre of Riga. To get there, take a *taksobuss* from the railway station or trolleybus number 8 from the Town Hall Square. Get off at the Graudu stop and you will find Turība 100m to the right. Singles Ls12, doubles Ls5.50, triples/quads Ls3/4 per person.

CAMPING

In 2004 a campsite opened on Ķīpsala island. It offers 63 places for tents and 20 places for trailers. It is also possible to play tennis and volleyball, rent roller skates and bikes, and have a meal. The campsite is around 20 minutes' walk from the Old Town. Lodging costs Ls1 per adult per night, and Ls0.50 per child. See www.bt1.lv/camping for more details.

Eating and drinking

Eating has been transformed in Riga over the past few years. Whatever your taste and whatever your budget, you should have no difficulty finding something to tempt you. Riga offers an immense selection of restaurants, cafés and bars, many up to the best international standards. In both the Old Town and the New Town Japanese and Chinese restaurants compete for custom with Italian, Russian, Ukrainian and, of course, Latvian restaurants. And if you just want a coffee or a snack, you won't need to walk far to find one of the many new coffee shops or tea houses. Wine is widely available in restaurants but is all imported and therefore not cheap. Beer is good quality and good value for money (see page 70).

In general you don't need to book in advance, although if you want to make absolutely certain of a table in a particular restaurant at peak times you could do so. Tipping has become increasingly the norm in recent years and 10% is considered about right for good service. Menus are nearly always available in English, so don't be afraid to ask if one doesn't appear automatically.

Prices tend to be low by western European standards but perhaps on the high side compared with some other eastern European cities. Main courses cost on average between £4–8/US$7–15 in upmarket restaurants, although more expensive dishes are also offered. A good two-course meal with wine for two therefore costs around £25–35/US$45–65. You can have a pizza for £2–3/US$4–6, or in some restaurants a small one for under £1.50/US$3. An ordinary white coffee will cost you around £0.50/US$1, although a latte or cappuccino could go up to £1.40/US$2.60. Many restaurants and cafés offer special lunch menus at very reasonable prices.

Latvian cuisine, if eaten regularly, is not for the weight-conscious. Once or twice on a weekend trip to Riga, however, it is an enjoyable and fun thing to try.

RESTAURANTS
Upmarket
Most of Riga's upmarket restaurants are in hotels. All of them are pleasantly decorated and all serve food to high standards, but the ambience depends very much on the clientèle. On a wet Monday out of season it is by no means unusual to eat alone in the evening in some of these restaurants, and although the staff do their best, it may be you would be happier in a livelier Old or New Town restaurant. On other occasions, the atmosphere might be just right, and there could be little more pleasant than the elegant dining these Riga restaurants offer.

Bellevue Maritim Park Hotel, 1 Slokas iela, tel: 706 9000
The 11th-floor restaurant looks out over the river on to the Old Town and is an ideal place for a sunset dinner in summer. The menu changes every month, so it is difficult to make recommendations. Fish and seafood are often among the highlights, and there are frequently local game dishes too. The décor, like everything else in this hotel, is modern, airy and elegant.

Restaurants

Bergs Hotel Bergs, in Berga Bazārs, 83/85 Elizabetes iela; tel: 777 0957 [1 C3]

Since the recent opening of the hotel, this restaurant has established itself as one of the best places to eat in Riga. The atmosphere is relaxed and the food includes a wide range of original dishes. The chef used to work at Vincents restaurant, where he achieved the high recognition he has now brought to Bergs. The Bergs serves lunch and dinner, and there is a breakfast buffet from 07.00–11.00; in the afternoon you can drop in for tea and cakes on the terrace.

LATVIAN BEER

For a small country Latvia has an awful lot of breweries, and it is not difficult to find many of the local brands at cafés and restaurants in Riga. Two of the most common beers, Aldaris and Cēsu, are now owned by foreign companies, Aldaris by Baltic Beverages Holdings, a joint venture between Scottish and Newcastle and Carlsberg, and Cēsu by the Finnish brewer Olvi, but most of the rest are pure Latvian, produced in local breweries in different parts of the country.

Beer (alus) is a traditional Latvian drink. There are many records of beer drinking in medieval times, when hop growing was also common. Over the last few years beer consumption has risen rapidly in Latvia: in 2003 average per capita consumption stood at 53 litres, almost double the level of the early

Otto Schwarz Hotel de Rome, 28 Kaļķu iela; tel: 708 7623 [3 D6]

Located on the top floor of the hotel, this is an international restaurant with an emphasis on German cuisine, including even a special asparagus menu in season. It is one of Riga's most established restaurants, but has lost none of its prestige as the number of competing restaurants has grown. A major advantage is the excellent views over the Freedom Monument and the parks. Prices are international, but at lunchtime there is a business menu for Ls8 (2 courses) or Ls10 (3 courses). A good choice of vegetarian dishes is always available too.

1990s, but even this level fades into insignificance in comparison with Finland, not to mention Europe's heaviest beer drinkers, the Czech Republic.

Aldaris is the brand leader in Latvia. Its Aldaris Zelta is widely available and has a taste similar to international brands such as Budweiser and Heineken. Cēsu Gaišais, from Latvia's oldest brewery in Cēsis, has a similar taste. If you'd like to try something a little different, you could look for Bauskas, Lāčplēšis, Piebalgas, Rigas, Tērvetes or Užavas. All of these brands are considered among the best in Latvia and all have distinctive tastes. Note that most brewers produce light (*gaišais*) and dark (*tumšais*) beer, so choose the brand and the type you would like. Piebalgas also produces the Minhauzena (Munchhausen) brand, which is slightly fruity and rather sweet. You can try all these beers at Rīgas Balzams (page 92).

LATVIAN FOOD

Traditional Latvian food is filling fare which fuelled farmers for their day's work. Unsurprisingly, given the dominance of German Balts in Latvia over the centuries, Teutonic cuisine has played an influential role. Standard items are many types of bread (see page 108), beans and peas, potatoes and sauerkraut, mushrooms and a wide variety of berries and fruits. Other typical food which you may encounter includes:

cūkas galerts (pork in aspic), often served with *etiķis* (vinegar) and *sinepes* (mustard) or with *mārrutki* (horseradish)

pīrāgi, small pies or pastries, probably originating in Russian cuisine, where they are called *pirozhki*. They have many fillings, but cabbage and boiled egg are traditional

skāba putra, cold soup, made from cracked barley, buttermilk, milk with sour cream

ķīsels, a thickened fruit soup (made from fresh berries) and often served with *buberts*, crème caramel

klingeris, a rich, yeast coffee bread in the shape of a pretzel, studded with raisins and almonds and flavoured with saffron and/or cardamoms: no Latvian birthday or other celebration is complete without this.

Rolands Hotel Rolands, 3a Kaļķu iela; tel: 722 0011[3 C6]

The medieval atmosphere of this cellar restaurant has been reconstructed by murals painted by Lila Dinere, a local artist, a covered well in the centre, and the heavy oak furniture. A nice touch (literally), particularly in winter, is the warmed table tops. Game dishes are what the restaurant has become known for, but it also serves fish, including eel, pork and other meat dishes. If available, try the confit of duck with vanilla pod potato mash and Cumberland sauce, or one of the dishes with a Japanese influence (shiitake mushrooms, udon etc). The hotel and restaurant were closed in late 2004 due to a legal dispute, but are expected to re-open.

Skonto Zivju Restorāns (Fish Restaurant) 4 Vāgnera iela; tel: 721 6713; www.zivjurestorans.lv [2 D6]

Riga's best fish restaurant is commensurately expensive and generally used by expense account diners. When we visited, the president was holding a private reception in a room at the back of the restaurant. There are 4 separate dining rooms, so wherever you are sitting the atmosphere is quiet and intimate. Fish is a mixture of local catch (try, for example, the Baltic Pike Perch Rolls as a starter) and of more exotic origins, and is always a pleasure to look at as well as to eat. Main courses go up to Ls17.00.

Vincents 19 Elizabetes iela; tel: 733 2634 or 733 2830; fax: 783 0206 [1 A1]

Vincents (the name comes from the van Gogh reproductions which decorate it) is one of Riga's best-known restaurants. Situated in the New Town, it offers a wide variety of dishes based on cuisines from around the world. Like many restaurants it is making increasing use

Restaurants

of high-quality local products, for example farm chicken from the Dobele region in western Latvia, but also has an impressive range of meat and fish dishes based on the best imported ingredients. A fairly recent addition is a sushi menu. It also has an attractive terrace for open-air eating in summer. Its reputation as a place where the 'stars' dine has led to very high prices by Riga standards. If you can't afford to go there, you can always try the menus on the website yourself: www.vincents.lv.

International

Palete 12–14 Gleznotāju iela; tel: 721 6037 [3 D7]

Located in an elegant building in a narrow street in the Old Town, the Palete is worth a visit. Despite its central location, it is often missed by tourists, so even in summer it tends to be uncrowded. Atmospheric and elegant with unobtrusive piano music, it's good value at about Ls12 per person for a full meal with wine; it is much less if you just have a snack. Dishes range from pasta to fried shellfish, chicken fillet with fried cheese and melon, and sometimes even rarer finds such as ostrich. The name means 'palette' and comes from its location in Painter Street.

Raibais Balodis (Colourful Dove) Konventa Sēta, 9–11 Kalēju iela; tel: 708 7580 [3 D7]

Part of the Konventa Sēta Hotel. Although the name may suggest a Latvian restaurant, the food here is definitely international. Menus change to make use of seasonal produce such as asparagus. The setting in the 13th-century convent is a definite plus, as are the fresh flowers and helpful service.

Melnie Mūki (The Black Monks) 1–2 Jāņa Sēta; tel: 721 5006 [3 D7]
Dark and rather formal, this highly respected restaurant in what used to be a cloister in the
Old Town is rapidly gaining popularity for international food at prices that, if high for Riga,
are by no means off the scale for the overseas visitor. The cuisine is genuinely international,
Turkish kebabs alongside dishes with Asian influences.

Italian

Da Sergio 65 Terbātas iela (entrance from Matīsa iela); tel: 731 2777 [1 D2]
A very Italian Italian restaurant, with a chef from Venice, many ingredients imported directly
from Italy, Italian music and Italian food and wine. The atmosphere is warm and welcoming
and puts you in the mood to enjoy everything from the bread, baked daily on the premises,
to the excellent desserts, via an interesting range of pizza, pasta, meat and fish main
courses. Prices are very accessible.

Pomodoro 81 Vecpilsēta iela; tel 721 1044 [3 D9]
Turn off Audēju iela with its crowds of shoppers into the peace of Vecpilsēta iela and you
will shortly find yourself at Pomodoro, a bar, café and restaurant. The restaurant is on the
ground floor of a 17th-century warehouse, and the décor is a mixture of traditional and
modern, but the mood is definitely contemporary. Pizza and home-made pasta are the
specialities, and the Italian owners ensure authenticity. Prices are very reasonable, and a
special children's menu is also available. Another branch has recently opened at the Domina
shopping centre (2 Ieriķu iela; tel: 787 3648).

Restaurants

Pizza

Pizza Jazz 15 Raiņa iela; tel: 721 1237 [1 B3]

The pizzas offered by this Lithuanian chain may not be the best you've ever tasted, but they are highly acceptable and eminently affordable. The menu has a large choice of pizzas, available in large or small size (and small really is quite small), as well as pasta and salad. Even large pizzas are only a little over Ls2. The main menu is in English as well as Latvian and Russian. The dessert menu isn't in English but there are enticing pictures. Try the biezpiena štūdele, cottage cheese strudel, if you fancy something with a Latvian flavour. Other branches are at 76 Brīvības iela, 19 Šķūņu iela and at the railway station.

Japanese

Planeta Sushi 16 Šķūņu iela; tel: 722 3855 [2 C5]

Owned by the Russian Rostik Restaurants group, like TGI Friday and Patio Pizza, and with branches in Moscow and other Russian cities, the pedigree for serving authentic Japanese food may not sound too promising. The quality of the vast range of Japanese dishes, however, comes as a very pleasant surprise. From miso soup to sushi (Japanese and Californian), teppan steaks or shabu shabu, the taste is first rate, and the prices quite reasonable too, with shrimp or squid sushi at only Ls1.20 per portion and teppan steaks at Ls5.00. The paintings of cherry trees on the wall and the Westernised kimonos worn by the waitresses are definitely less authentic, but the overall ambience is pleasant, unhassled and comfortable, and the location, close to Dome Square, makes this a convenient and highly recommendable spot.

Latvian

Dzirnavas (The Mill) 76 Dzirnavu iela; tel: 728 6204 [1 C3]

One of the most popular of Riga's restaurants among locals, this Latvian farmhouse-style restaurant is not the place for a quiet tête-à-tête. The service is buffet-style: choose from a vast array of food laid out in several rooms, take it back to your table, across the stream in the centre, and enjoy it to the strains of Latvian country music. The food is decent, the atmosphere fun, and the prices very affordable. If you want a quick initiation into Latvian food and at the same time to observe local life, this is a good place to start.

Lido Atpūtas Centrs (Lido Recreation Centre) 76 Krasta iela; tel: 750 4420

This is undoubtedly one of Riga's recent success stories in the restaurant world. To take over an out-of-town estate rather than a house in an area barely accessible by public transport required considerable daring but the gamble has paid off as the crowded car park proves every evening. Family groups are the main target, as large play areas are available, and service is cafeteria-style with trays along the counter. More and more foreigners are now coming too; they enjoy, as the Latvians do, the space, the light and the wooden tables, not to mention the variety and quality of food available in the bistro, express restaurant or beer cellar with its own micro-brewery. They enjoy the broad clientèle too; Latvia mixes here in a way it hardly does elsewhere. The centre also has the largest skating rink in the Baltics. To get there take tram 7 or 9 to the Dzērvju stop. It's then a 10-minute walk towards the windmill. Alternatively take a short taxi ride (Ls2–3).

Restaurants

Livonija 21 Meistaru iela; tel: 722 7824 [3 D6]

There are few restaurants in Riga where an identical review could be written year after year. For the Livonija, this is the case and it has always been positive. Nothing changes, and why should it? A broad international menu, with a wine list to match, is offered, although there is a good choice of Latvian dishes. Acclaimed dishes include local venison, pork knuckle, smoked eel and lamprey. The service remains unobtrusive and the art nouveau chairs will never be forgotten. The restaurant is in a cellar well underneath the hurly-burly of Livu laukums; this position shelters it not only from noise but also from the climate: it stays cool in summer and warm in winter.

Vērmanītis 65 Elizabetes iela; tel: 728 6289 [1 B3]

If Latvians meet each other, this is often the place they will choose. Prices are certainly not 'Old Town' and it manages to bridge the generation gap better than many other restaurants. Probably the self-service elements and the wooden dance floor help to do this. Older folk will be soothed by the stained glass and stone in much of the decoration. It is supposed to recall the first independence period from 1920 to 1940. Pizza and salad are always popular dishes here amongst foreigners but Latvians stick to the dependable local meat dishes.

Russian

Arbat (named after an area in Moscow) 3 Vāgnera iela; tel: 721 4056 [3 D6]

This is probably the most upmarket Russian restaurant in Riga, although the prices, for the quality of the food, are not at all unreasonable. Caviar, sturgeon and vodka feature prominently on the menu and blend well with the richly ornate interior. The dishes are attractively presented by staff who are unusually keen to please. If you have always wanted to know what it would feel like to be a character in *War and Peace*, a visit here will help you imagine it.

Krievu Sēta/Russkij Dvor (The Russian Courtyard) 3 Ķengaraga iela; tel: 713 4930
This is the Russian equivalent of the Latvian-food Lido restaurant, and owned by the same group. A huge building in an unfashionable part of the city, off Maskavas iela (Moscow Street), the interior resembles a theme park, with its painted wood and traditional matroshka dolls. Like the Lido it offers a self-service restaurant with a massive choice of dishes and a recreational area outside. The food includes Russian favourites such as borscht, blini, solyanka and pork, all at low prices. Tram number 7 or 9 from opposite the Opera will take you there. Alight at the Ķengaraga iela stop.

Traktieris 8 Antonijas iela; tel: 733 2455 [1 A2]
Hearing Russian and Ukrainian spoken here by other diners is clearly a good sign. The Russia to which this restaurant wants to link is of course the one that died in 1917, not the later variant that died in 1991. Although in the heart of the art nouveau area, the décor is from rural Russia, as are the costumes worn by the staff. The menu is from aristocratic St Petersburg and includes staples such as blini and borscht as well as more unusual dishes, but the prices appeal to quite a range of classes. In 2002, a buffet was opened, presumably for architecture fanatics determined to miss nothing in the surrounding neighbourhood, but a stay of at least 2 hours is recommended in the main restaurant.

Restaurants

Ukrainian

Spotikačs 12 Antonijas iela; tel: 750 5955 [1 A2]

Unless you visit Ukraine there are not many opportunities to sample the cuisine. This restaurant will give you a good idea of what's eaten in Kiev: straightforward, tasty dishes, with plenty of meat, potatoes and vareniki (dumplings). The floral friezes and puppets give the décor a childish feel and, added to the friendly service, should make your visit here a happy experience. If you need any further help, try the chilled home-made vodka. A branch has also opened in Jūrmala (see page 201).

Chinese

Hongkonga 61 Valdemāra iela; tel: 781 2292 [1 E1]

What a relief to find a Chinese restaurant in the Baltics where what you see is what you get. The ambience is straightforward but the cooking more elaborate. It is clear that Chinese are in control of the whole operation and are catering for their colleagues; if others wish to come, they are welcome to have a meal that makes no concessions to so-called Western tastes.

Indian

Sue's Indian Raja 3 Vecpilsētas iela; tel: 721 2614 [3 D9]

This is one of Riga's few Indian restaurants, but would be likely to be one of the best even if it had lots more competitors. The food is authentically Indian and includes tandoori and tikka dishes as well as curries. Thai dishes are also available. The camels that feature on the door are possibly a reference to the fact that Indian spices, transported by camel on part of their journey, used to be stored in a warehouse here. Prices are not low, but the quality of food and service is worth paying for. There is also a branch of the restaurant in Jūrmala (see page 201).

Vegetarian

Kamāla, 14 Jauniela; tel: 721 1332 [3 C5]

An Indian ambience suffuses the restaurant: you'll notice the incense before you enter, and once inside the colourful table and wall decorations will transport you beyond Riga. The menu too features Indian food fairly strongly, but a range of other dishes is also available. Recommendations are difficult as the menu changes from day to day but you will always find a number of very appealing, and rather different, options, including perhaps tofu shashlik (bean-curd kebab).

Jamaican

Coco Loco 6 Stabu iela; tel: 731 4265 [1 C2]

The only Jamaican bar and restaurant in Riga (although there is now also a branch in Jūrmala – see page 199), Coco Loco is a colourful and lively venue, offering Jamaican and other Caribbean dishes in generous portions and at very affordable prices. If you like reggae music, this will be paradise: reggae plays every day, but on Fri and Sat nights from 20.00 the restaurant becomes a club with DJs putting on the music. As you might expect, there is also a choice of trendy cocktails. Although slightly out of the centre, this area around Stabu iela is enjoying something of a renaissance. Close to Coco Loco is the Sarkans restaurant, a branch of Zen café and also of Double Coffee.

Restaurants

Quick snacks

Blinoff 30 Brīvības bulvāris [1 B3]

If you want to replenish your energy between the Old Town and the New Town, call in at Blinoff. This small but welcoming café offers a long list of *blini* for Ls1–2. Choose from sweet or savoury *blini*, with coffee or a soft drink.

Sievasmātes Pīrādziņi (Mother-in-law's pīragi) 10 Kaļķu iela [3 D6]

Pīragi (Latvian pasties) and cakes are baked here on the premises and sold for as little as Ls0.08. Good quality and very popular. You can afford several, and a juice (no alcohol available) as well, and still have plenty of money left in your pocket.

Pīrādziņi 14 K Barona iela; tel: 728 7824

A *pīragi* (Latvian pasties) shop offering pasties with a wide range of fillings from cabbage to meat. An excellent snack if you're in a hurry in the New Town.

Cheap and filling

Pelmeņi XL 7 Kaļķu iela; tel: 722 2728 [3 D6]

It's not sophisticated, but it certainly won't leave you either hungry or bankrupt. Pelmeni are rather like ravioli, but their Russian origin means they're more substantial. You can fill up your plate with an XL portion from a choice of six different types (chicken, pork, vegetarian etc), and accompany the main dish (Ls1.50) with soup and salad. There is a similar ambience, but bigger choice, at Pelmeņi, 38a Čaka iela.

Eating and drinking

RIGA 24

As the number of nightclubs has expanded, a new market in 24-hour eating has grown up with it. If you want to eat in the small hours, and room service does not oblige, you could try one of the following:

Lauvas Nams (Lion House) 82 Brīvības iela, tel: 729 7645. A large buffet and grill.

Lido 54 Ģertrūdes iela. Good, solid Latvian food.

Melnais Kaķis (Black Cat) 10/12 Meistaru; tel: 751 7011. Reasonably priced food and drink, plus video games and slot machines (closed 07.00–09.00).

For 24-hour shops, see page 109. For 24-hour pharmacies, see page 32.

Olé 1 Audēju iela; tel: 722 9563 [3 B8]
Another buffet-style café, which, despite the name, serves international, not Spanish, food. Take as much as you can eat and you should still have change from Ls3.00.

Breakfast alternatives

If you fancy a change from hotel breakfasts, you won't need to go far to find interesting alternatives. All the options below are open from 08.00 Monday to Saturday. On Sundays you'll have to force yourself to have a late breakfast.

Restaurants

Ai Karamba! 2 Pulkveža Brieža iela; tel: 733 4672 [1 A1]

In the New Town, close to the art nouveau area. Cereal, eggs and pancakes. Sun from 10.00.

Dzirnavas (The Mill) 76 Dzirnavu iela; tel: 728 6204 [1 C3]

Also in the New Town, this restaurant which later in the day offers a Latvian buffet also offers a breakfast buffet with all you could desire, for Ls2.50. Closed Sun.

John Lemon 21 Peldu iela; tel: 722 6647 [3 B8]

In the Old Town, close to the Ainavas Hotel. A range of breakfast menus, some healthy, some less so, in pleasant surroundings. Sun from 10.00.

I love you 9 Aldaru iela [2 D3]

For only LS1.49 you can help yourself from a small breakfast buffet in this Old Town café. Sun from 10.00.

CAFÉS

For **internet cafés**, see *Internet*, page 41.

Café Opera Aspāzijas bulvāris [1 B4]

A suitably ornate café has been inside the Opera House since it opened in 1995, with plenty of marble and wood. It never advertises, which suits the regulars who prefer the peace and quiet and the absence of tourists even in July and August. A thick soup followed by a light salad makes a good lunch here. The café has an outside terrace too – with parasols which appear at the first drop of rain.

Lidojošā Varde 31a Elizabetes iela at the corner of Antonijas iela; tel: 732 1184 [1 A1]
'The Flying Frog' serves simple food (omelettes, pasta, salad, hamburgers) at very
affordable prices, as well as drink. Popular both in summer, when you can sit on the
terrace, and in winter, when a fire glows in the hearth. Handy when exploring Riga's art
nouveau buildings.

Coffee and tea

A new generation of coffee and tea houses has arrived in Riga in the last few years.
Gone are some of the traditional Viennese-style cafés, to be replaced by an ever-
growing choice of cappuccino bars and tea houses. Wherever you are in central
Riga, you will never have to go far for a high-quality coffee or a mouth-watering
cake. Chains of coffee shops have emerged, but they have not (yet) been joined by
the international chains so well known elsewhere. An unusual feature in most
coffee shops (although not in Coffee Nation) is that take-way coffee costs a little
more than drinking in the café.

Coffee houses

Monte Kristo 18/20 Kalēju iela, close to Konventa Sēta; tel: 722 7443 [3 D7]
Also at 27 Ģertrūdes iela and 10 Elizabetes iela. At once spacious but cosy, this high-class
coffee house offers a very wide choice not only of coffee but also of tea. Cakes include an
enticing berry tart, excellent warm and with cream.

Cafés

Double Coffee 11 Vaļņu iela, on the corner of Kaļķu iela; tel: 712 3522
Also at 40 Brīvības iela, 25 Raiņa iela, 15 Stabu iela, 52 Barona iela. Always busy, with good reason. The cafés offer an immense choice not only of coffee, tea and chocolate, but also of sandwiches, cakes, omelettes and even sushi. The extensive menu is fully illustrated, so it's easy to pick out exactly what you'd like. Prices are very reasonable too, with a single cappuccino available for well under Ls1.

Coffee Nation 4 Tirgoņu iela [3 C6]
Also at 21 Valdemāra iela, 5 Blaumaņa iela, 24/26 Barona iela and Stacijas laukums (Station Square). Another popular coffee-house chain, serving a selection of coffees, as well as some snacks and sandwiches. The chain is owned by Latvians, but is modelled on Starbucks and was the first in Riga to offer American-style coffee-to-go.

Kafijas Veikals (Coffee shop) 6 Mazā Pils iela; tel: 722 42 16 [2 C3]
Now an exception in Riga, this Viennese-style café is small, popular and one of the best for coffee and cakes. Unfortunately it is closed on Sat and Sun as well as in the evenings. Open 08.30–18.00 Mon–Fri.

Charlestons Cappuccino Bar 38/40 Blaumaņa iela; tel: 777 0573 [1 C2]
A popular café with locals, who enjoy the coffee and the range of sandwiches, cakes and salads. If you're in Riga long enough, a loyalty card will make your 7th cup of coffee free.

Emihla Gustava Shokolahde 13/VI Marijas iela (in Berga Bazārs); tel: 728 3959 [1 C3]
Also at 24 Aspāzijas bulvāris (in Valters un Rapa bookstore). Essentially handmade chocolate

shops, but you can also have coffee, or chocolate, watch Belgian-style chocolates being made (at the Berga Bazārs) and enjoy a chocolate or two with your coffee. The cappuccinos are large and extremely frothy, the service very friendly, and the prices rather on the high side for Riga.

Tea houses

Aspara Tea Rooms 22 Skārņu iela, tel: 722 3160 [3 D7]

In the historic Ekke's convent built in 1435 as a guesthouse for travellers (page 123), this tea house offers a relaxing ambience in the heart of the Old Town. In the basement you can sit on cushions and choose from a vast array of Japanese, Chinese and Indian teas, while upstairs the décor is European medieval. Another branch is located in a small wooden house in the Vermānes Garden (opposite house number 75 on Elizabetes iela). Other branches also at 10 Šķūņu iela, 77 Valdemāra iela and 2 Terbātas iela.

Zen 6 Stabu iela; tel: 731 6521; www.zen.lv [1 C1]

This will definitely not be your cup of tea if you are just looking for a refuelling stop. Enter Zen and you enter a slow-motion world which you will need some time to enjoy. Chinese tea is prepared in ceremonial style and, authentically, takes at least 20 minutes. The décor is oriental too: tatami, cushions, candles and lanterns, though – slightly out of kilter with the rest of the place – waterpipes are also available.

Cafés

7 Entertainment and nightlife

OPERA AND CONCERTS

The Latvia National Opera (3 Aspazijas bulvāris; tel: 722 5803; fax: 722 8240; email: boxoffice@opera.lv; www.opera.lv [1 B4]) has an extensive programme of opera, ballet and recitals. Ticket prices are extremely reasonable by international standards, tending to range from Ls2–30, although international stars may sometimes dictate higher prices. Tickets can easily be booked from outside Latvia via email, and then collected at the ticket office (slightly behind the main building, towards the park) on arrival in Riga. Even if you do not book in advance, it is often possible to buy tickets once you are in Riga. Performances are normally in the original language but surtitled in English and Latvian where necessary. Programmes are in Latvian and English. An opera festival is held every year in June. This can be booked directly or as part of an opera tour (page 24). Unfortunately the opera is closed in July, August and much of September. Inside the opera is Café Opera, a peaceful haven of wood and marble, which offers a pleasant venue for a snack and is open even in July and August when the theatre is closed.

The Latvia National Opera has an extremely high reputation and over the years has attracted a wide variety of well-known musicians and designers. Richard Wagner conducted over forty operas during his time in Riga (1837–39), although in the forerunner to the current building, which was not built until 1863. He also wrote a large part of *Rienzi* while he was here, and it is said that he conceived some of the motifs for *The Flying Dutchman* on a journey from Riga to Copenhagen. More recently Bruno Walter spent several years conducting at the Opera House. Although many performances are of the classical repertoire, there is a strong tradition of contemporary dance, and the choice of operas is often bold, including for example in 2004 a revival of Anton Rubinstein's little-known *Demons*.

Classical concerts are held in a variety of venues, including the **Wagner Hall** (Vāgnera Zale) (4 R Vāgnera iela; tel: 721 0817 [3 D6]), the **Great Guildhall** (Lielā Ģilde) (6 Amatu iela; tel: 721 3798) and the **Small Guild Hall** (Mazā Ģilde) (3–5 Amatu iela; tel: 722 3772 [2 D5]). Organ and other chamber recitals are given regularly at the **Dome Cathedral**, Doma laukums [2 C5], usually on Wednesdays and Fridays. Tickets can be purchased just inside the porch of the main entrance. In all these cases, there is generally no need to pre-book, unless the artist is extremely well-known. Other venues also host occasional performances: if you keep your eyes open when walking around Riga you will see adverts for up-coming events. The free city guides also give a selection of concerts with details of time and place. Information on music in Riga generally can be found at www.lmic.lv.

Venues for non-classical music are more varied. For blues, one of the most highly recommended places is **Bites Blūzs Klubs** (34a Dzirnavu; tel: 733 3125), which frequently attracts singers from the USA and elsewhere. **Sapņu Fabrika** (Dream Factory) (101 Lāčplēša iela; tel: 729 1701; email: info@sapnufabrik.com) is a large hall which puts on a variety of world music, jazz and rock concerts. **The Hamlet Club** (5 Jāņa Sēta; tel: 722 8838) hosts jazz concerts, and also serves as a small

Opera and concerts

theatre, putting on plays which often have a strong political content. For a genuine Latvian experience, try **Četri Balti Krekli** (Four White Shirts) (12 Vecpilsētas iela; tel: 721 3885; www.krekli.lv), which specialises in Latvian musicians, including for example Ainars Mielavs (page 101).

Every summer the **Rigas Ritmi** festival (www.rigasritmi.lv) is held in Riga in June/July. It attracts well-known musicians from around the world, who not only perform but also give masterclasses. The music is wide-ranging, including reggae, world music, bossa nova, jazz'n'soul and Caribbean. Venues include open-air performances in parks and squares in Riga and even on cruise ships on the Daugava.

FILMS AND THEATRE

Riga offers a number of state-of-the-art cinemas, all of which show films in the original, rather than dubbed, so visitors will have no problems viewing missed Hollywood films. Seat prices are low by international standards at an average of Ls2.0–2.70, but even so discounts are offered on weekday showings before 17.00. Information on what's showing can be found at www.filmas.lv (in Latvian but comprehensible to English speakers: click Afiša on the top horizontal for film times and locations), on the individual websites indicated below, by phoning 722 2222 or checking one of the city guides.

With 14 screens, **Forum Cinemas** (www.baltcinema.lv) is the largest cinema in Riga and the second-largest cinema complex in the whole of northern Europe. It is located at 8 Janvāra iela, more or less at the end of Aspāzijas bulvāris [1 4B], and has all the modern facilities you would expect. Other possibilities include **Daile** (31 Barona iela; tel: 728 3843; www.baltcinema.lv [1 C3]), which shows older films for just Ls1.20 per person; **K Suns** (83/85 Elizabetes iela; tel: 728 5411 [1 B3]), which tends to show European, rather than Hollywood films; **Kinogalerija** (24 Jauniela; tel: 722 9030 [3 B5]) which specialises in classics; and **Riga** (61 Elizabetes; tel: 728 11 95 [1 B3]), the first cinema to open in Riga and recently renovated in its original style but with modern equipment.

Riga has a number of theatres but most of these are inaccessible to visitors who do not speak Latvian or Russian. For those who do, the **New Riga Theatre** (25 Lāčplēša iela; tel: 728 0765; www.jrt.lv) tends to perform avant-garde plays in Latvian, while the **Russian Drama Theatre** (16 Kaļķu iela; tel: 722 4660 [3 D6]) does what it says. The **National Theatre** (2 Kronvalda bulvāris; tel: 732 2759; www.teatris.lv – Latvian only [1 A3]), housed in a classical building close to the canal, performs a primarily classical repertoire. It was here that Latvia declared independence on November 18 1918. A concert is held here every year to commemorate the event. For more information, see www.theatre.lv, which gives information in English as well as Latvian.

Of possible interest is the **State Puppet Theatre**, based at 16 Kr Barona iela (tel: 728 5418; email: info@puppet.lv; www.puppet.lv [1 C3]). The puppet theatre is a strong Latvian tradition and performances are generally well acclaimed. They are in Latvian or Russian, but visitors with a particular interest may appreciate the artistry.

BARS AND CLUBS

Riga's night scene has blossomed in the last few years. It now offers a huge variety of venues and entertainments to suit all tastes and most pockets. The venues below are only a very small selection of what is on offer. For up-to-date listings in this rapidly changing area, see one of the bi-monthly Riga guides.

Pulkvedim Neviens Neraksta (Nobody Writes to the Colonel) 26–28 Peldu iela; tel: 721 3886 [3 B8]
One of the longest-established clubs in Riga, this is also one of the city's trendiest venues, regularly crowded with young locals and visitors – but seems to have no connection with the Márquez novel of the same name. The food is generally well liked, although the service can be slow. If you like sitting in a warehouse listening to alternative music, this is for you. If you prefer something more colourful, go down to the **Baccardi Lounge** in the basement of the same building, and enjoy cocktails to the accompaniment of disco house, but be warned that if you're over 20 you may well be the oldest there.

Rigas Balzāms Building 1b at 4 Torņa iela in the Jēkaba Kazarmas row of shops near the Powder Tower; tel: 721 4494 [2 D3]
If you'd like to try Riga's distinctive alcoholic drink, Rigas Melnais Balzāms (Black Balsam), is a good bar to visit. We would recommend trying it first in a fruit cocktail. The faint-hearted can choose from many better-known drinks. The bar also serves pub-type food, and the pleasant ambience makes it a popular place for Rigans relaxing after work – and well into

the evening. The same management have now opened a second bar, Jaunais Rigas Balzāms at 2 Doma Laukums (Dome Square).

Skyline Bar (in Reval Hotel Latvija) 55 Elizabetes iela; tel: 777 2222 [1 B2]
One of the best views in Riga can be had from the Skyline Bar on the 26th floor of the Reval Hotel Latvija. Take one of the 2 glass-sided lifts up to the top and enjoy a beer or a cocktail with all Riga spread below you.

Vairāk Saules Cocktail Bar (More Sun) 60 Dzirnavua iela; tel: 728 2878 [1 C3]
One of the longest cocktail menus in Riga (around 90) won't prevent you being stunned by the brightness of the décor in this trendy bar. The music is mostly R&B and the service better than in many bars. It is a popular venue with locals, so make sure you arrive early if you want a seat.

Paldies Dievam Piektdiena Ir Klāt (Thank God it's Friday) No 9, 11. Novembra krastmala; tel: 750 3964 [1 A4]
Closed on weekdays until the eponymous Fri, this weekend bar offers a taste of the Caribbean on the banks of the River Daugava. Everything about the bar transports you across the Atlantic: the food, including Cuban black bean soup, the reggae music, the barman in shorts, the flamboyant cocktails and, on Fri and Sat, women dancing on the bar.

La Habana 1 Kungu iela; tel: 7226014 (entrance from Rātslaukums, Town Hall Square) [3 C6]
On the upper floor this is a quiet restaurant serving Tex-Mex dishes. The basement is quite different. From Thu to Sat, it turns into a popular disco hosted by local DJs. The rest of the

week Latin music predominates, as you'd guess from the decoration – pictures of Che Guevara, Fidel Castro et al.

Voodoo (part of Reval Hotel Latvija) 55 Elizabetes iela; tel: 777 2355; www.voodoo.lv [1 B2] This newly revamped club is open from Thu to Sat from 20.00–05.30. It offers several dancefloors, quieter areas for drinking and a lively atmosphere. It attracts many Russians, partying in Riga, as well as locals. Admission at Ls3–5 is good value.

GAY RIGA

Although the legal restrictions which the Soviet authorities imposed have long since disappeared, the gay scene is not yet well developed in Riga. Open affection in public is rarely seen and may attract hostility. Only two gay clubs are widely advertised:

Purvs (The Swamp) 60–62 Matīsa iela; tel: 731 1717; www.purvs.lv. Open 22.00–24.00; Fri and Sat 22.00–6.00. Closed Tue. Admission Ls1–4
Generally well reviewed, if you can find it – there is no sign. It offers dance performances, sometimes including transvestite shows.

XXL 4 A Kalniņa iela; tel: 728 2276; email: xxl@xxl.lv, www.xxl.lv. Open 18.00–7.00 every day, but men only on Sun. Admission Ls1–10 [1 C4]
XXL started life as a small bar but has now expanded into a larger club and restaurant, with shows on Fri and Sat at 03.00. Video cabins and dark rooms are also available.

For further information, contact Gays and Lesbians Online, tel: 727 3890, email: gay@gay.lv, www.gay.lv (in Latvian only). A new website is also currently under construction: www.gaybaltics.com.

Shopping

Riga offers every type of shopping experience, from state-of-the-art shopping malls and boutiques to street stalls and markets. Despite the low cost of living, international fashion brands are in general expensive compared with many other European cities, so don't expect to pick up bargains. On the other hand, most everyday items, food and drink, and most of the things you might think of buying as presents, are modestly priced in comparison with western Europe or the USA.

Many, but not all, small shops close on Sundays, but the shopping centres are open seven days a week. During the week small shops tend to be open from 10.00 or 11.00 until 18.00 or 19.00, while most of the shopping centres are open from 10.00 to 22.00. A number of mini supermarkets and pharmacies are open 24 hours a day (pages 32 and 109).

Although there are shops all over Riga, the two major areas are in the Old Town, particularly for gifts, and the New Town area, close to the Reval Hotel Latvija.

PRESENTS FROM RIGA

If you're looking for gifts to take home to friends and family, Riga offers a wide selection of products which are distinctively Latvian and distinctly different from the normal run of souvenirs, including:

- Amber: many different qualities and colours, from almost clear lemon to dark brown, are available (see page 102).
- Riga Black Balsam (see below)
- Laima chocolates
- Wooden toys and utensils
- Latvian folk costumes or dolls in national costume
- Latvian linen

RIGA BLACK BALSAM

For something that is uniquely Latvian, be sure to pick up a bottle of *Rigas Melnais Balzāms* (Black Balsam), a thick, black drink with a bitter taste, marketed as a medicinal tonic. Supposedly it calms the nerves and is good for an upset stomach. Production of *Melnais Balzāms* was begun in the 1700s in Riga. To this day the exact recipe is a closely guarded secret, but the ingredients (over 25 in all) include: 16 grasses, ginger, oak bark, bitter orange peel, lime blossom, iris roots, nutmeg, peppermint, valerian, brandy and sugar. It is sometimes mixed with vodka or (more recently) Coca-Cola. The distinctive brown ceramic bottle in which it is sold is as well-known in Latvia as the drink itself. If you'd like to sample before purchase, have a drink at Rigas Balzāms (page 92).

Presents from Riga

- Latvian vodka
- Latvian music
- Soviet memorabilia
- Bread and cheese (see page 108)

ANTIQUES

Note that generally a licence from the Inspection Board for History and Culture and the Protection of Monuments is needed before you can export antiques or valuables. There are no customs duties if goods are exported to EU countries, and reduced rates are payable on export to certain designated countries (for example, Australia, Canada and Russia). For further information, consult the Board at 22 Pils iela; tel: 721 4100.

Most shops will also help you with the paperwork.

Whilst antiques are available in the Old Town, most shops are off Brīvības iela, fairly near to the Reval Hotel Latvija.

Antikvariats 8 Baznīcas iela [1 B2]
Mainly deals in paintings and clocks but also has a few books.

Antiqua 20 Kr Valdemāra iela; tel: 728 4377 [1 B2]
Paintings and other fine art.

Doma Antikvariats 1a Doma Laukums (Dome Square); tel: 722 1056 [2 C5]
Furniture, paintings, porcelain and other high-priced items. If you can read Russian, more information is available at www.antikvariats.lv.

Galerija 53 Dzirnavu iela; tel: 728 2978 [1 C3]
Not really antiques – more mementoes of the Soviet era, plus books, coins and similar small items.
Konvents 9/11 Kaļķu iela (in Konventa Sēta); tel: 708 7542 [2 D6]
Paintings, icons, porcelain and antique furniture.
Raritets 45 Čaka iela; tel: 727 5157 [1 D2]
Interesting selection of porcelain, furniture, paintings and icons.
Volmar 6 Šķūņu iela; tel: 721 4278 [2 C6]
Two floors of paintings, icons, furniture, old musical instruments and other antique items.
Also at 46 Brīvības iela; tel: 728 3436 and at 9/11 Kalēju iela; tel: 708 7542.

ART

Riga has a large number of contemporary art galleries with regularly changing exhibitions where it is possible to purchase local artworks. Most are in the Old Town.

Birkenfelds 6 Amatu iela; tel/fax: 721 0073 [3 D5]
Carousell 2 Kaļķu iela; tel: 721 0487 [2 D6]
Ivonna Veiherte 9 Pils iela; tel: 722 2641 [2 B3]
XO 8 Skārņu iela (in Konventa Sēta); tel: 948 2098 [2 D7]

BOOKS

Globuss (Vaļņu iela 26) and **Valters un Rapa** (Aspāzijas bulvāris 24) are almost side by side, opposite the Riga Hotel and with just the post office in between.

Valters un Rapa is probably the largest bookshop in the Baltics. It also sells CDs, and films (including Fuji Velvia). A branch of Emihla Gustava Shokolahde is located on the ground floor, where you can buy coffee, tea or hot chocolate, and choose handmade chocolates to accompany them. Globuss concentrates on travel books. **Jāņa Sēta** (Elizabetes iela 83–85) are best known for their maps which cover the whole Baltic area. They produce country maps, town plans and atlases. Prices for their own publications tend to be cheaper at their shop than elsewhere. Their catalogue can be consulted on www.kartes.lv. **Jumava** (Vāgnera iela 12, close to the Konventa Sēta Hotel) has a wide selection of antiquarian books in German, English and French, many about Latvia and Riga. The **War Museum** in the Powder Tower has a wide selection of books, many in English, about the build-up to independence in the late Soviet period. The **Museum of the Occupation** also sells books in English relating to the occupation.

Globuss 26 Vaļņu iela; tel: 722 6957 [3 D9]
Specialises in travel books.
Jāņa Rozes 5 Kr Barona iela; tel: 728 4288; www.jr.lv [1 C3]
Also at 90 Brīvības iela, in Dole shopping centre (tel: 727 4556); at Audēju iela 16 in Centrs shopping centre (tel: 701 8092); at Basteja iela 12 in the Mols shopping centre (tel: 721 0080); 46 Krasta iela (tel: 703 0331); and in the Origo shopping centre at the railway station (tel: 707 3169).
Jāņa Sēta 83–85 Elizabetes iela; tel: 724 0892 [1 C3]

Jumava 73 Dzirnavu iela; tel: 728 2596; www.jumava.lv [1 C3]

Has a café and a good stock of foreign-language books. A branch at 12 Vāgnera iela sells second-hand books, including many in German, French and English, about Riga and Latvia.

Valters un Rapa 24 Aspāzijas bulvāris; tel: 722 9294 [3 D9]

MUSIC

CDs and cassettes are cheap, but watch out for pirated and counterfeit products. If you would like to take home something distinctively Latvian, look for folk music, organ music from the Dome Cathedral or perhaps the music of Imants Kalniņš, a contemporary Latvian composer who has worked in a wide variety of forms from symphonies to rock'n'roll, or of Ainars Mielavs (see below).

Randoms 4 Kaļķu iela; tel: 722 5212 [2 C6]

Claims to be the largest music shop in the Baltics. Two floors of Latvian, world and pop music (ground floor) and heavy metal (basement).

Upe (River) 5 Vāgnera iela [2 D6]

Sells traditional Latvian instruments and cassettes and CDs of Latvian music. Upe is owned by Ainars Mielavs, a well-known figure in the Latvian music industry, who has worked with the Latvian band Jauns Mēness (New Moon), and who appears frequently on local television and radio.

Music

SOUVENIRS

Many amber sellers have stalls in the Old Town, notably near the Dome and in Vālņu iela. Products are of variable quality, so you need a good eye for genuine value if you decide to shop here.

A & E 17 Jauniela; tel: 722 3200 [3 B5]
Specialists in amber, particularly designer jewellery. Visiting dignitaries such as Hilary Clinton are always taken here. Prices reflect this customer base, but you can rely on the quality.

AMBER

Amber is formed from the resin which oozed from pine trees some 30 to 90 million years ago and gradually fossilised. It is found in several parts of the world, but the oldest source, some 40–50 million years old, is in countries around the Baltic Sea, including Latvia. The use of Baltic amber goes back a very long way: amber of Baltic origin has been found in Egyptian tombs from around 3200BC, and Baltic amber was regularly traded in Greek and Roman times. Animal figurines made of amber have also been found in Latvia dating back to the 4th millennium BC. After the Teutonic Order conquered Latvian territory, local people were forbidden to collect it on pain of hanging and only in the 19th century could inhabitants of the coast

Domiņa 3 Maiznīcas iela; mob: 921 9032

Wooden toys and games for children and adults. Custom orders also taken.

Grieži 1 Mazā Miesnieku; tel: 750 7236 [2 B4]

More than just a shop selling linen, ceramics and jewellery. Demonstrations of craft-making (Mon) and traditional cooking (Thu). Best to telephone in advance to check.

Koka Varde (Wooden Frog) 31 Lāčplēša iela; tel: 728 2063 [1 C2]

A good place to go for wooden souvenirs, many from the Sigulda area north of Riga, as well as for linen and other souvenirs.

once again begin amber-working.

Traditionally Latvian folk costumes made use of three items made from amber: beads, brooches and *kniepkeni* (fastening for women's blouses). All of these items, and many others, can be found in shops in Riga. Are they all real natural amber? Definitely not. Unfortunately the only recommended test to establish authenticity is hardly a practical shopping tip: make a solution of water and salt and drop in your amber. Only real amber will float.

Dzintars, the Latvian word for amber, can be seen and heard all over Riga. It is the name of Latvia's main perfume company, a brand name for a cheese spread, the name of a well-known choir, a children's dance group, and is also a common first name (Dzintars for men and Dzintra for women).

Souvenirs

Laipa 2/4 Laipu iela; tel: 722 9962 [2 D6]
Handmade linen tablecloths, napkins and towels, plus
woollen items, jewellery and other souvenirs. Weaving
demonstrations too.

Livs 7 Kalēju iela; tel: 722 9010 [2 D7]
Like Laipa, specialises in linen and jewellery, often fashioned on
traditional Baltic designs. Weaving demonstrations.

Māra 9–11 Kalēju iela (in Konventa Sēta); tel: 708 7541 [2 D7]
A wide choice of amber products, as well as linen. If you are
visiting Māra you can also have a look at **Rota**, also in Konventa
Sēta (tel: 708 7546), which sells amber, ceramics and a range of small
Latvian gifts.

Amber

Nordwear 7 Kaļķu iela; tel: 784 3546; www.nordwear.com.lv [2 D6]
Advertises itself as 'amber-free'. It has a number of humorous souvenirs (mugs, T-shirts etc),
but its main speciality is hand-knitted sweaters, based on traditional Latvian symbols. You
can obtain a 5% discount card from many hotels, so there is no need to pay the full price.
See the website for the shop's full catalogue.

Sakta (Brooch) 32 Brīvības bulvāris; tel: 728 0868 [1 B3]
This was Riga's first souvenir shop and dates back to Soviet times. Offers a wide variety of
gifts, including amber, linen and Rigas Balzāms. Prices tend to be lower here than in some of
the Old Town shops. Another smaller branch at 30 Aspāzijas bulvāris (tel: 722 7751),
between the Riga and Metropole hotels.

Shopping

Senā Klēts 13 Merķeļa iela; tel: 724 2398 [1 B3]
Specialises in folk costume from the different regions of Latvia. If they don't have one that fits you, they are happy to make one.

Vecpilsēta 7–9 Kaļķu iela; tel: 722 5427 [2 D6]
Amber jewellery, ceramics and some paintings.

CHOCOLATES

Laima chocolates (www.laima.lv) have been made in Riga since 1870. You can find them at speciality shops 22 Miera iela, 16 Smilšu iela, 16 Marijas iela and at other branches in Riga, and also in supermarkets, where they tend to be cheaper. The classic Luxs bar with red rose design is a long-standing favourite. For a more indulgent present, try the cranberry liqueur chocolates (Prozit) or the beautifully presented Riga selection.

Emihla Gustava Shokolahde 13 Marijas iela (in the Berga Bazārs [1 C3]), in Valters un Rapa bookshop (café and shop) and in many shopping centres around Riga.
These handmade Belgian-style chocolates are a relatively new, and very welcome, arrival in Riga.

FLOWERS

Flowers are particularly close to the hearts of most Latvians: you will see people welcomed at the airport with flowers, and people walking to work or going home, clutching small bunches. They are on sale in markets and on the street throughout Riga, generally at very low prices. The main **Flower Market** is at the side of Vērmanes Garden on Tērbatas iela [1 B3], but you will make one of the many people standing on the street selling their own flowers very happy if you buy a small bunch for your hotel room.

SPECIALITY SHOPS

Ballera Kanceleja 13 Marijas iela (in Berga Bazārs) [1 C3]
Handmade paper and stationery.

Latvijas Balzāms 1 Marijas iela; tel: 722 8715 [1 C3] and other branches in Riga.
More than 50 different types of Latvian alcoholic drinks, including the well-known Black Balsam.

Latvijas Bite 13 Ģertrūdes iela; tel: 727 9495 [1 C2]
The honey shop of the Latvian Association of Beekeepers specialises in honey and related products. Branches also at 34b Dzirnavu iela and 1a Kalniņa iela.

SHOPPING CENTRES

The last few years have seen an explosion of shopping centres in Riga. Joining Centrs, which has survived many rebirths since the 1920s, has come a range of large malls such as you can find in most capitals anywhere in the world.

Centrs 16 Audēju; iela tel: 701 80 18 [3 D8]
In the heart of the Old Town. Since renovation in the 1990s, the previous department store

has been reborn with a Rimi supermarket on the ground floor, plus four other floors with clothes shops, restaurants, cafés and a pharmacy.

Mols 46 Krasta iela; tel: 703 0300

American-style mall with clothes shops, supermarket, coffee shops and sushi bar. Located on the banks of the Daugava, a short walk in time, but at least a century in mood, from Maskavas iela. A free minibus service (clearly marked Mols) operates to and from the station.

Origo 2 Stacijas laukums; tel: 707 3030 [1 B4]

This huge shopping centre engulfs the new railway station to such an extent that you may have difficulty finding the platforms. A massive choice of shopping and eating possibilities of a far higher quality than often lurk around stations.

SUPERMARKETS

Rimi In Centrs at 16 Audēju iela in the Old Town; tel: 701 8020 [3 D8]

In most shopping centres.

Stockmann No 8, 13 Janvāra iela [1 B4]

On the ground floor of this recently opened Finnish department store is a large supermarket with an extensive and much praised delicatessen.

MARKETS

Riga's indoor and outdoor markets are great fun to walk round. The largest by far is the Central Market (Centrāltirgus), but if you are passing, the Vidzemes market in the New Town is also worth a quick look. The Central Market sells a huge array

BREAD

Bread in all its forms, from sweet varieties to sour dough, is a great favourite with Latvians. Many areas of the country have their own special bread recipes, and although the industry is currently undergoing some consolidation you can still find many regional variations. Jelgava Maiznieks (the bakery of Jelgava, a town to the west of Riga), for example, has branches in Riga, and in the Central Market you will find many more local breadmakers.

If you'd like to try something different, look out for dark rye bread (*ista rupjmaize*), a traditional Latvian bread, baked in a wood-fired oven and containing no additives. The long fermentation process means that the bread can be kept for up to three weeks and also that the vitamins in the bread are better for you than additives. It is often known now as *Lāči* (bears), the name of one farm bakery which has revived the traditional method of making the bread, and which now even exports large loaves (at 8kg this gives a new meaning to the concept of a large loaf) to the USA.

The bread can be found in most food shops and at the Central Market in Riga (Centrāltirgus). With local caraway cheese, *ķimeņu siers*, it makes a filling lunch-time snack.

of food of all types, as well as clothing, hardware and more or less anything you can imagine.

Centrāltirgus (Market) 1 Prāgas iela; tel: 722 9981 [1 B4]
Close to the railway station
Vidzemes Tirgus 90a Brīvības iela; tel: 731 1796 [1 D1]

24-HOUR SHOPS
Avots Food, drink and a delicatessen. 22 Čaka iela; tel: 728 1828
Delikatesen 7 Šķūņu iela; tel: 722 2706 [2 C5]
Kalissa 4 Ģertrūdes iela [1 C2]
Visbija Small supermarket. 68 Brīvības iela; tel: 727 5190 [1 C2]

Walking tours

The majority of sights are in the Old Town (Vecrīga), the area of the city located between the Daugava River and the city canal (*pilsētas kanāls*). If your time is limited, this is the place to start. If you have more time, you could include a look at the art nouveau area. For visitors with still more time or other interests, a number of other walks in and around the centre are described below.

The Old Town contains a wealth of historic buildings, from the medieval town walls dating back to the 13th century to the grey modernity of the flats and offices built when Latvia was part of the Soviet Union. Between the two extremes there are buildings of almost every period and style, classical, Gothic, art nouveau and modern. Much of the Old Town suffered neglect when Latvia was part of the USSR, but a great deal of restoration and reconstruction has now been undertaken (the reconstruction of the Blackheads' House and surrounding area being one of the most striking examples).

The best way to see the Old Town is on foot: the area is relatively small, but in any event, large parts of the Old Town have been made traffic-free zones (there is access for vehicles, but you have to buy a pass), while other parts consist of narrow streets, making vehicle access impractical. Many of the streets are cobbled and others suffer from lack of maintenance, so you have to keep your eyes open for holes and uneven road and pavement surfaces. Wear sensible walking shoes.

The main sights of the Old Town are described below by reference to two suggested walking routes covering the Old Town sights on either side of Kaļķu iela.

OLD TOWN: WALK ONE

Our first walk starts from the Hotel de Rome at the corner of Kaļķu iela and Aspāzijas bulvāris [3 DC], not far from the Freedom Monument. Walk down Kaļķu iela away from the Freedom Monument and the parks along the side of the hotel and you will find yourself almost immediately at Vaļņu iela, a pedestrianised street of shops, bars and cafés. Turn right into Vaļņu iela. At the end of the street you will see one of the major landmarks of the Old Town, the **Powder Tower** (Pulvertornis, page 177 [2 C4]). This sturdy tower is all that remains of the 18 towers which once formed part of the city walls. You may wish to visit the **War Museum** (Latvijas Kara Muzejs, page 164), which the Tower now houses. If not, stand on Smilšu iela (Sand Street), one of Riga's oldest streets, with your back to the Powder Tower and look across Basteja bulvāris where you can see the remains of **Bastion Hill** (*Basteja kalns*), one of the fortification towers dating back to the 17th century.

Behind the Powder Tower is Torņa iela (Tower Street), a well restored, traffic-free street. Walk along this street and you come to part of the city wall (best seen from the parallel Trokšņu iela). Riga was protected by a wall from the early 13th century. Eventually it extended to a length of over a mile. By the 14th century the walls were 1.83m thick. The arches between the pillars would be filled with stones

Old Town: walk one

and sandbags to provide reinforcement when the city was under siege; in peacetime they were emptied again and used for storage or as stables or even accommodation. The income derived from letting the arches was used to raise money to pay for the upkeep of the city's defences.

At the corner of Torņa iela and Aldaru iela (Brewer Street) is the **Swedish Gate** (*Zviedru Vārti* [2 D3]), so called because it was built when Riga was under Swedish rule and because it was the gate through which the Swedish king, Gustavus Adolphus, entered the city in 1621 (a stained-glass window in the Dome commemorates this). It is the only city gate still left intact. According to legend, the citizens of Riga abducted a young Latvian woman who had unwisely fallen in love with a

Swedish Gate

Swedish soldier and was meeting him secretly near the gate, and walled her up in the gate as a warning to others. The Swedish Gate is unusual in that it passes through a whole house (number 11 Torņa iela). The house at number 11 is the first recorded house in private ownership in Riga.

Although it is not possible to visit them, there are several attractively restored historic houses on Torņa iela of which the most notorious is the one now at number 7, a large pink house that was once occupied by the city executioner until the position was abolished in 1863. Number 5 Torņa iela was the site of the prison built in 1685 by Rupert Bindenschu, the architect who also worked on the reconstruction of St Peter's Church.

At the end of Torņa iela you come to Jēkaba iela (Jacob or James Street) and to the right **Jēkaba laukums** (Jacob's or James's Square), where concrete barricades were erected during the struggles of January 1991. The square, which was first laid out in the 18th century, was once used for military parades and exercises. On the side of the square closest to Jēkaba iela is a row of low buildings. The middle building, taller than the others, is the former arsenal. Built between 1828–32 to designs by I Lukini and A Nellinger on the site of what was once part of the town wall, the arsenal that stood here was replaced by a customs house. Now the building is a gallery (the **Arsenal Museum of Fine Arts**, Mākslas Muzejs 'Arsenals' [2 C2]) where modern painters exhibit (page 146).

Close to the end of Torņa iela is a green which forms part of **Pils laukums** (Castle Square). The large building on the corner on your right is the Bank of Latvia, built in 1905 to designs by the Latvian architect, Reinbergs. Number 2 Pils laukums was formerly a Red Army museum but is now the **Museum of Writing, Theatre and Music** (Rakstniecibas, Teatra un Muzikas Muzejs, page 165). The main building on Pils laukums, at the other side of the square, is **Riga Castle** (Rigas pils [2 B2]), a large cream building with a red roof (page 178), where the President of Latvia now lives.

The castle also houses two museums, the **Latvian History Museum**, Latvijas Vēstures Muzejs (page 152), which traces the course of Latvian history from 9000BC to the 20th century; and the **Latvian Museum of Foreign Art**, Latvijas

Ārzemju Mākslas Muzejs (page 152), the biggest collection of foreign art in Latvia. To the right of the castle, in the direction of Kr Valdemāra iela, is the old stable block, recognisable by horse-head designs on the wall.

Leaving Castle Square (Pils laukums) and crossing the cobbled area of the square (the opposite end to the one at which the stables are located, in the direction of Lielā pils iela) you come to a church, the Roman Catholic church of **Our Lady of Sorrows** (Sāpju Dievmātes baznīca, page 170). Just beyond the Catholic church is Riga's only Anglican church, **St Saviour's** (page 175 [2 B3]) , which stands in Anglikāņu iela, just off Lielā pils iela. The church was built for the British community in 1859 and became a discothèque during the Soviet occupation, but is now restored and holds regular Sunday services. On a fine day the outdoor café at the end of Anglikāņu iela offers views over the river and the imposing Vanšu bridge, and makes a pleasant stop. The tall building on the far bank is the Hansa Bank 26-storey office building.

Returning to Pils iela, go back to the corner of the square and turn right into Mazā pils iela, heading away from the tower of Riga Castle. The three houses at numbers 17, 19 and 21 Mazā pils iela are known collectively as '**the three brothers**' (Trīs brāļi, page 179 [2 C4]). Note also the house at 4 Mazā pils iela where the Baltic historian Johans Kristofs Broce worked from 1742–1823 as rector of what was then Riga's imperial lycée.

Opposite 'the three brothers' is Klostera iela (Monastery Street) which leads to **St Jacob's,** or **St James', Church** (Jēkaba baznīca, page 171 [2 C3]), the Roman

Catholic cathedral of Riga, and the church with the lowest of the three spires which dominate the Old Town.

At the corner of Jēkaba baznīca, if you turn right, you come to a formidable brown building with a coat of arms and a balcony over the main entrance. This is the building where the Supreme Soviet of Latvia used to sit. Between 1919–34 it was the seat of the **Latvian National Parliament** [2 C3]. Now it functions once again as the parliament building, the seat of the Saeima. It was here on May 4 1989 that parliament passed a resolution on the independence of Latvia. The building itself is in the style of a Florentine palace. Note the decoratively carved double doors and heavy lanterns. In the outbreak of crime which followed independence in the early 1990s, the bronze plaque on the front of the building was stolen.

Turn right into Jēkaba iela and walk along the back of the cathedral. Numbers 6–8 Jēkaba iela form a substantial stone building which houses the **Latvian National Library** [2 C3]. Designs by the Riga-born architect Gunars Birkerts for a new national library, to be known as Gaišmaspils (the 'Castle of Light'), so far remain on the drawing board. Turning left back into Smilšu iela, the house at number 6 has a modern front and is now a bank. The upper storeys are good examples of the art nouveau style of architecture for which Riga is so famous. The buildings at number 2 and number 8 are also worth a look. Next to number 6 is Aldaru iela (Brewer Street) with its view back to the Swedish Gate. The large brown building that dominates the rest of Smilšu iela is occupied by ministries and government offices.

Old Town: walk one

House of the Cat

Here the road forks. Take Mazā Smilšu iela (Little Sand Street) and turn right into Meistaru iela (Master Street). On your left is a large yellow building called the **House of the Cat** [2 C5]: perched on each of the building's two pointed towers is an arched cat looking down on the city. The origins of this piece of architectural caprice are uncertain but inevitably there is a story. Apparently a Latvian businessman sought admission to the city guild but was refused. To spite the guild he bought the nearest land he could find to the guildhall, built the house that still stands and had two cats put on top so that each directed its backside towards the guildhall. According to the same story the spurned merchant was eventually forced to move them, hence their present position.

If you continue down Meistaru iela you come to what used to be the Guild Square but is now known as the **Philharmonic Park** (Filharmonijas Parks). On a wet day it can look fairly grim but in better weather it is enlivened by kiosks selling ice-cream and drinks, and by pavement artists. The **Great Guildhall** (Lielā Ģilde, page 176 [2 D5]) is the large, dull yellow building at one edge of the square, at the corner of Meistaru iela and Amatu iela (Commercial Street). The **Small Guildhall** (Mazā Ģilde) is right next to it on Amatu iela itself. These buildings represent the centres of Riga's former glory as a Hanseatic City. Continue along Amatu iela to Šķūņu iela (Barn Street). On your right there is a camel-coloured building with white decoration, an excellent example of Riga's art nouveau. Note the sculptures of a boy reading (at roof level) and of frogs (by the entrance).

If you turn right out of Amatu iela, past Zirgu iela, you come to the Cathedral Square, Doma laukums. The square is dominated by the cathedral, the **Dome Church** (Rigas Dome – the word comes from the German *Dom*, meaning cathedral, page 166 [2 C5]) or St Mary's Cathedral, as it is sometimes referred to, the largest church in the Baltic states. The church has restricted opening hours for tourists (page 166), but there are also opportunities to attend concerts there on Wednesdays and Fridays, frequently featuring the cathedral's splendid organ, and services are held at 08.00 every day and at noon on Sundays. Close to the main entrance and away from the main square, is the **Cross-Vaulted Gallery of the Dome** (page 168), the cathedral cloister and courtyard now in the final stages of restoration. This can be visited daily and has good views of the Dome exterior.

Just off Doma laukums, Tirgoņu iela (Traders' Street) has a number of bars and restaurants. Behind the Dome is Jauniela (New Street): the **Pūt, Vējiņ!** is a good place to eat and drink (there is a bar downstairs and a good restaurant upstairs).

The building at 8 Doma laukums is the **Latvia Radio Building** [2 C4]. It and the nearby Finance Ministry recall the architectural style of Nazi Germany and were built during the time of the Latvian president, Kārlis Ulmanis. The Radio Building was one of the buildings that was barricaded in 1991 by demonstrators resisting communist sympathisers; bullet holes in the building offer a grim

Old Town: walk one

reminder of the fighting. Doma laukums was heavily guarded and occupied by people lighting bonfires and erecting tents. From time to time radio staff would appear on the balcony of the Radio Building to announce the news to the people gathered in the square below. It was from the same balcony that President Gorbunovs proclaimed independence in August 1991. Opposite the Radio Building is Rigas Fondu Birža, the **Riga Stock Exchange** [2 C4], a green and brown building with ornate statues. It was built in 1852–55 in Venetian style to a design by the architect Harald Bose, fell into disuse during the Soviet occupation but during the 1990s was again occupied by a bank.

If you leave Doma laukums passing the main door of the cathedral with the Radio Building behind you, you come into Herdera laukums, **Herder Square** [2 B5]. This small square is dominated by the statue of the German critic, writer and theologian, Johann Herder, who lived in Riga from 1764–89. Turning out of Herdera laukums you come to Palasta iela (Palace Street). The building that was once the clergy enclosure of the abbey attached to the Dome is now the **Museum of History and Navigation of the City of Riga** (Rigas Vēstures un Kuģniecības Muzejs, page 154 [2 B5]). Further on in Palasta iela at number 6 stands a tiny building in which the Russian tsar, Peter I, kept his personal carriage when he visited Riga. Just beyond it at number 9 is what used to be **Peter I's palace**, from which Palasta iela derives its name. In 1745 the palace was rebuilt to designs by Rastrelli, the architect better known in Latvia for his work on the Rundāle Palace (page 205).

OLD TOWN: WALK TWO

Our second walk in the Old Town starts from the beautifully restored Rātslaukums (Town Hall Square) towards the end of Kaļķu iela near the river [2 B6].

The distinguished building dominating the square is the **Blackheads' House** (Melngalvju nams, page 149), rebuilt in 1999. Although the ornate exterior is the most stunning aspect, the interior can also be visited. Particularly impressive is the assembly hall on the first floor. If you have any questions about Riga, you can visit the Riga tourist information office housed in part of the Blackheads' House. Next to the museum entrance there is a small café, where the brave can sample Vecriga coffee (coffee with balzāms). While on the square, have a look at the **statue of Roland** (page 184) and also at the newly restored **Town Hall** (Rātsnams) opposite the Blackheads' House.

After the medieval atmosphere of the Town Hall Square, the aggressively 20th-century atmosphere of the Riflemen's Square (Strēlnieku laukums) next to it towards the river comes as something of a shock. The large statue is the **Memorial to the Latvian Riflemen** (page 180) which was erected in 1970 to commemorate the valour of the Latvian Rifle Regiment during the civil war. The ugly black cuboid building behind the memorial was also built in 1970 and used to be a museum devoted to the exploits of the regiment. Now it is the **Museum of the Occupation of Latvia**

Memorial to the Latvian Riflemen

Old Town: walk two

(Okupācijas Muzejs, page 158). The museum offers a detailed and poignant account, with many personal histories, of the various occupations Latvia was subjected to during the 20th century.

The traditional bridge with the large lantern-like lights is the **Akmens tilts** (Stone Bridge) which replaced the long pontoon bridge that spanned the river before World War II. A more elegant example of 20th-century architecture is the dramatic modern bridge, the harp-like **Vanšu tilts**, which crosses the river to the north.

Leave the square by turning into Grēcinieku iela (Sinner's Street) and taking Kungu iela (Gentleman's Street). On the corner of Grēcnieku iela and Kungu iela is the **Mentzendorff House** (Mencendorfa nams, page 155 [3 C8]). The house once belonged to a rich Riga merchant family and is now a museum of life in the 17th and 18th centuries. Walk down Kungu iela past the Mentzendorff House to Mārstaļu iela. Number 21 Mārstaļu iela is (or will be, once restored) a fine example of baroque domestic architecture and was built in 1696 for another wealthy citizen of Riga, Dannenstern and his family. Nearby at number 19 is a plaque to George Armisted (1847–1912), a Scot who was lord mayor of Riga city. (If you are traveling more widely in Latvia, you can see the manor house he built, Jaunmoku Pils, just outside Tukums.) The red house at number 2 Mārstaļu iela is the **Reiter House** (Reitera nams), built in 1682 for another wealthy Riga merchant, Johann von Reiter, and now used for conferences and exhibitions.

Turn right into Audēju iela (Weaver Street) and then right again into Vecpilsētas iela (Old Town Street). The buildings at numbers 10 and 11–17 are good examples of some of the 20 or so medieval warehouses of the old town. On the corner opposite the Italian restaurant is the house from which the **Latvian Popular Front** operated in the late 1980s and which is now a small museum (page 160 [3 D9]). Return to Audēju iela and continue walking away from Mārstaļu iela. The street is normally packed with shoppers, but if you have chance glance up over the door of number 3. Next to the German motto 'God protect our going in and going out' you will see **storks** on a nest. Storks are a striking feature of rural Latvia, where the 6,000 or 7,000 pairs which arrive annually are welcomed by local people as bringers of good luck. Throughout Latvia, including in the ballroom decoration at Rundāle (page 208), you will find the stork motif.

Turn left into Rīdzene iela, alongside the Centrs shopping centre, then left again into Teātra iela (Theatre Street), which brings you to Kalēju iela. Just off Kalēju iela is a passage leading to the **Konventa Sēta** [3 D7], an area of beautifully restored historic buildings between Kalēju iela and Skārņu iela. The area, which dates back to the 13th century, now contains a hotel, shops and the **Porcelain Museum** (Rigas Porcelāna Muzejs, page 161). Close to the Konventa Sēta at the end of Teātra iela there is a part of the city wall. An archway in Kalēju iela leads to Jāņa Sēta (John's Courtyard), a cobbled courtyard with the city wall on one side and a bar, café and restaurant forming the other sides of the quadrangle.

A second arch leads out of the courtyard to **St John's Church** (Jāņa baznīca, page 171 [3 D7]), with its wonderful vaulted ceiling inside and intriguing stone faces outside.

RIGA STREET NAMES

An easy way to learn some simple Latvian words, and also to learn more about Riga's history, is to take note of the street names. In the Old Town, the names tend to focus on the street's original use. In the New Town, streets are often named after famous Latvians. For reference, *iela* = street, *laukums* = square and *bulvāris* = boulevard.

Old Town

Akmens	Stone	Kalēju	Blacksmiths'
Aldaru	Brewers'	Klostera	Monastery
Alknāja	Alder	Krāmu	Odds and Ends
Amatu	Commercial	Kungu	Gentlemen's
Audēju	Weaver	Palasta	Palace
Gleznotāju	Painters'	Peldu	Pig
Grēcinieku	Sinners'	Pils	Castle
Jaun	New	Skārņu	Butchers'
Kaļķu	Lime	Šķūņu	Barn

Skārņu iela (Butchers' Street) got its name from the shops that were located in this part of Riga in medieval times. Number 22, next door to St John's Church, is a

Smilšu	Sand	Tirgoņu	Merchants'
Torņa	Tower	Trokšņu	Noise
Vecpilsētas	Old Town	Zirgu	Horse

New Town

Note that in the Latvian language even people's names change their endings to agree with the word which follows. Raiņa iela, for example, would be Rainis Street in English.

Rainis	Latvian poet (see page 203) and husband of:
Aspāzija	Latvian poet and wife of Rainis
K Ulmanis	Latvian president during the first period of independence
Kr Barons	Collector of folksongs (see page 148)
Valdemārs	A leader of Latvia's National Awakening (see pages 5 and 154)
Lāčplēsis	Legendary hero (see page 183)
Blaumanis	Latvian artists (see page 125)

house known as **Ekes konvents** (Ekke's Convent). The building is currently a tea-house. Further along Skārņu iela, next to number 10, the old white building with brick-lined windows is **St George's Church** (Jura baznīca), possibly the oldest building in Riga and generally dated at 1202 or 1204. In 1989 it became part of the **Museum of Decorative and Applied Arts** (Dekoratīvi Lietišķās Mākslas Muzejs, page 151), which specialises in applied art from Latvia and abroad from the 19th century onwards. Opposite Ekke's Convent in the shadow of St Peter's there is a modern statue of some animals called *The Town Musicians of Bremen*. Based on an old German tale, it is a gift from the city of Bremen to the people of Riga and marks a long association between the two cities.

On the other side of Skārņu iela stands one of Riga's most famous and distinctive churches, **St Peter's** (Pētera baznīca, page 173 [3 C7]), a large red-brick church with a simple, light interior decorated by coats of arms. St Peter's is the tallest spire in Riga. Except on Mondays you can take a lift up to the viewing platform and have a spectacular view of Riga. On leaving St Peter's, return to Skārņu iela and then turn right into Kaļķu iela. This last part of our walking tour of Old Riga will take you past some of Riga's newest shops and bring you back to the Hotel de Rome and a sign that Riga is now a thoroughly 21st-century consumer-oriented city: opposite the hotel and almost in the shadow of the Freedom Monument is what was Riga's first McDonald's.

ART NOUVEAU WALK

Riga has one of the largest collections of art nouveau buildings in the whole of Europe. Around one-third of all the buildings in central Riga were built in this style between around 1896 and 1913. Even if you did not think you were interested in architecture, it is worth having a look at a few of the most striking examples – which may make you change your mind. In this case, you can integrate a quick tour of the art nouveau area within the New Town walk (see below). Visitors more interested in buildings could easily spend a half day exploring the area in more detail and visiting the Jānis Rozentāls and Rūdolfs Blaumanis Memorial Museum (see page 163).

Although art nouveau buildings are to be found throughout the New Town, as well as in certain parts of the Old Town, the area with the most striking buildings is the rectangle bounded by Elizabetes iela, Antonijas iela, Alberta iela and Strēnieku iela [1 A1]. Also of interest are many of the buildings along Brīvības iela, Lāčplēša iela, Ģertrūdes iela, A Čaka iela and Terbātas iela, all in the main New Town shopping area.

Wandering around these areas, and remembering to look up to the very top of the buildings, gives an idea of the range of styles and the sheer inventiveness of many of the architects. Some of the most memorable buildings are the work of Mikhail Eisenstein (1867–1921), father of film director Sergei of *Battleship Potemkin* fame. These include **10b Elizabetes iela**, with its monumental faces, and the well-restored building at 41 Strēnieku iela, now occupied by the School of Economics. Numbers 2, 2a, 4, 6 and 8 and 13 Alberta iela are also his work. Number 4 is of particular interest. With lions dramatically astride the turrets, it was for several years

ART NOUVEAU IN RIGA

Within the relatively short time when art nouveau flourished in Riga various sub-styles can be distinguished: eclectic art nouveau, perpendicular art nouveau and from 1905 the distinctively Latvian National Romanticism.

Art nouveau (or Jugendstil as it is known in German) originally developed in Germany and Belgium towards the end of the 19th century and spread rapidly throughout Europe as far as Spain and Hungary. Its original decorative elements – birds, animals, shells, elaborate flower motifs are typical – were in stark contrast to the academic styles of the late 19th century. Philosophically, art nouveau introduced the concept that everything useful should be beautiful; the outside of a building for example should be suited to the function of the building. As the style spread throughout Europe individual countries developed their own variations.

The style which developed in Riga was influenced mainly by German, Austrian and Finnish architects, but the approach also has distinctive elements drawn from Latvian cultural traditions and construction techniques. Most of the architects who designed Riga's art nouveau buildings were trained at the Riga Polytechnical Institute; almost 90% were Baltic Germans, but the 10% or so of native Latvian architects built about 40% of the new buildings.

The most extravagant art nouveau buildings are in Alberta iela. Five of the apartment blocks here (numbers 2, 2a, 4, 6, 8) were designed by Mikhail Eisenstein. Close by, Elizabetes iela is also rich in art nouveau buildings, including the former studio of the painter Jānis Rozentāls, now a museum. The building was designed in 1904 by Konstantīns Pēkšēns (one of the most prolific art nouveau architects, responsible for over 250 buildings). The spectacular murals lining the circular staircase inside the building bear witness to the fact that art nouveau was not limited to building exteriors, but also included interior design, furniture, china, glassware and book design.

After the revolution of 1905 a distinctively Latvian variation of art nouveau developed, known as National Romanticism. Keen to promote national awareness at a time of oppression, architects sought to use traditional Latvian folk art elements and to use the language of the indigenous art of wooden construction. Natural building materials were used, and typical elements were steep roofs, heavy structures and the use of ethnographic ornamental motifs. Some examples include Brīvības iela 47, Terbātas iela 15–17 and Kr Valdemāra iela 67, all built by Eižens Laube (together with K Pēkšēns in the case of the school building at Terbātas iela 15–17).

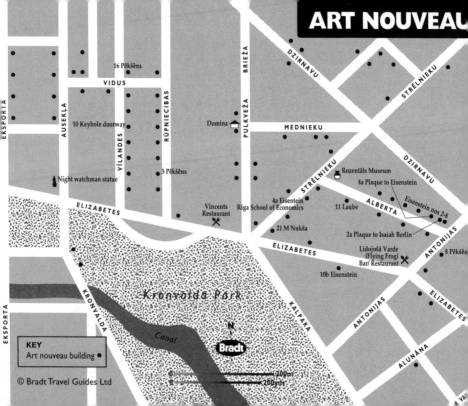

ART NOUVEAU

KEY
Art nouveau building •

© Bradt Travel Guides Ltd

16 Pēkšēns

VIDUS

10 Keyhole doorway

Night watchman statue

3 Pēkšēns

EKSPORTA

AUSEKĻA

VILANDES

RŪPNIECĪBAS

BRIEŽA

DZIRNAVU

STRĒLNIEKU

PULKVEŽA

MEDNIEKU

Domina

STRĒLNIEKU

DZIRNAVU

Rozentāls Museum

4a Plaque to Eisenstein

4a Eisenstein

11 Laube

ALBERTA

Eisenstein nos 2–8

Riga School of Economics

ELIZABETES

Vincents
Restaurant

21 M Nukša

2a Plaque to Isaiah Berlin

ANTONIJAS

8 Pēkšēn

ELIZABETES

Lidojošā Varde
(Flying Frog)
Bar/ Restaurant

10b Eisenstein

ELIZABETES

KRONVALDA

Kronvalda Park

Canal

KALPAKA

ANTONIJAS

ELIZABETES

ALUNĀNA

EKSPORTA

N

Bradt

0   100m
0   200yds

the home of Eisenstein. At number 12 Alberta iela, designed by Konstantīns Pēkšēns, is the **Jānis Rozentāls and Rūdolfs Blaumanis Memorial Museum** (Jāṇa Rozentāla un Rūdolfa Blaumaṇa Memoriālis Muzejs, page 163). The museum is an interesting record of the lives of the painter and the writer, but even if you do not visit the museum, it is worth looking into the entrance and admiring the elaborate staircase.

Other buildings of note in this area include the block at the corner of Strēlnieku iela and Elizabetes iela (21a) which has a plaque to commemorate the architect and diplomat Mārtiņš Nukša (1878–1942), 23 Elizabetes iela, with the motto 'Labor vinvit omnia' ('Work conquers all'), numbers 3 and 14 Ausekļa iela, and numbers 3 and 4 Vidus iela.

While Eisenstein's buildings are in the eclectic art nouveau style, the buildings in the New Town shopping area reflect a greater diversity of styles. Examples of perpendicular art nouveau can be seen at 49–51 Terbātas iela, the work of Eižens Laube, and at 61 Lāčplēša iela (architect Rudolf Dohnberg). One of the first National Romanticism buildings is at 4 Lāčplēša iela, an apartment block designed by Pēkšēns and built in 1905.

Although the majority of art nouveau buildings are in the New Town, there are some in the Old Town as well. There are examples at Smilšu iela (number 8, the cake shop; number 6, a bank; and number 2, designed by Pēkšēns); Sķūnu iela (number 4 and 12–14); there is an imposing doorway opposite the Pūt, Vējiņ! restaurant at 25/29 Jauniela (architect Wilhelm Bockslaff), and a more colourful example at 23 Kalēju iela, the work of Paul Mandelstamm. The attractive Flower House, with paintings of pharmaceutical plants on the outside walls, is at the corner of Mazā Monētu iela and Mazā Jaunava, just behind the Rolands Hotel.

NEW TOWN WALK

The Old Town and New Town are separated by the city canal (*pilsētas kanāls*) which runs through a series of parks and gardens. The canal follows the line of part of the old city wall which was demolished in the 19th century. Through the centre of the parks, separating the Old Town from the New Town, is Brīvības bulvāris (Freedom Boulevard), a pedestrianised street that is also the site of the Freedom Monument. This is where the New Town Walk starts [1 B3].

The **Freedom Monument** (Brīvības piemineklis, page 181) dominates the centre of Riga and has played a central and symbolic role in Latvia's chequered history. Close to the Freedom Monument (on the Old Town side of the park) stands the **Laima clock**, another landmark and a popular meeting point. Laima is the name of a well-known chocolate manufacturer and the Latvian word for happiness or good luck (there was an ancient deity of that name).

Southwest of the Laima clock is a fountain, the Nymph of Riga, which dates back to 1888. It stands in front of the stately **National Opera** [1 B4], the home of Riga's opera and ballet companies. Originally built as a German theatre, this impressive building (classical on the outside, baroque on the inside) can be seen from anywhere in this central parkland area. Founded in 1919, the National Opera was the focus of Latvian cultural life during the first independence and has resumed an important role in recent years (page 88).

The Opera House is a good starting point for strolls through the parks in the centre of Riga, either through **Bastejkalns Park** (page 185 [1 A3]) with its memorial to five victims of the events of 1991, through **Kronvalda Park** (page 185) with its monuments to Latvian writers, Riga Congress House (Rigas kongresu nams) and the Riga Council Building (Rigas dome), or beyond the Freedom Monument towards the New Town, through **Vermānes Park** (page 186 [1 B3]) or the **Esplanade Park** [1 B2].

A number of interesting buildings are scattered in or around the parks. These include **Riga University** on Raiņa bulvāris, a Gothic building with elements of the Romanesque. It stands on the site of the ancient Rīdzene River, long since channelled underground, and was originally used by the Riga Polytechnical Institute. It features a stone staircase divided into three parts, the centre section of which is traditionally used only by graduates. On Merķeļa iela, the street behind the university and alongside Vermānes Park, is the impressive **House of the Riga Latvian Society** (Rigas Latviešu Biedrība [1 B3]). The society was founded in 1868 at a time when Latvian was fighting to become a widely acknowledged language but the current building, with paintings on the façade by Jānis Rozentāls, dates from 1910. Just opposite, say hello to the engaging **statue of Kārlis Padegs**, an artist whose scandalous paintings were the talk of Riga in the 1930s (page 181). At the north end of the Esplanade Park on K Valdemāra

WOODEN BUILDINGS

Although still not very well known internationally, Riga's wooden buildings have aroused a great deal of interest locally in recent years, and with justification. Wooden architecture developed over many years in Riga, almost until World War II, long after most countries in Europe had turned away from it. In the post-war period, when wooden buildings in many countries were destroyed, buildings in Riga were left intact, mainly because of the lack of housing under Soviet occupation. Since the restoration of independence there has been a trend among wealthier people to buy and renovate some of these lovely buildings, most of which had fallen into disrepair.

The oldest surviving wooden buildings are from the middle of the 18th century and are in Pārdaugava (the opposite bank of the river from the Old Town). The best preserved example of 18th century is perhaps the Hartman estate (Hartmaņa muižiņa) at 28/30 Kalnciema iela (west of the intersection with Slokas iela). Another example is 28 Daugavgrīvas iela, although most buildings from this period are still in poor condition. A well-preserved example from the early 19th century is the Blok estate (Bloka muižiņa) on the corner of Vienības gatve and Altonavas iela south of Torņakalns station. Estates such as this had a country atmosphere about them, although they were situated on one of the main roads into Riga. Unfortunately very few examples still exist.

An easily accessible area where wooden buildings abound is the Maskavas district, and in particular Maskavas iela. If you take tram number 7 from the stop opposite the National Opera you will go through the Central Market and emerge a little later on Maskavas iela (see page 136). Most of the wooden houses here are from the end of the 19th and beginning of the 20th century. Typically they are large two-storey residences, some with gables and cornices. At 149–153 Maskavas iela, near Maskavas dārzs (park), for example, you can see a row of such houses.

Wooden buildings are also scattered around the New Town. At the time when art nouveau was in fashion, many Latvian architects were interested in building in wood as well as in stone. Examples can be found at 100 Brīvības iela (in the courtyard, designed in 1899 by K Felsko), on Ernesta Birznieka-Upīša iela, near the station, and at many other locations. Inside some of the wooden buildings, some fine interiors and staircases have survived.

See also Mežaparks (page 143) and Jūrmala (page 193) for examples of wooden buildings.

New Town walk

Kārlis Padegs statue

iela stands the **Academy of Art** (Mākslas akademija), a fine example of neo-Gothic architecture. In front of it there is a statue by Burkards Dzenis (1936) of Jānis Rozentāls, the founder of the Latvian Realist school of painting. Next to the Academy is the **State Museum of Art** (Valsts Mākslas Muzejs, page 146 [1 B2]) , built in 1905 by Wilhelm Neumann in German baroque style, which houses a collection of 17,000 paintings. If you are not making a separate trip to examine the **art nouveau area** (page 124) in detail, here would be a good point to make a quick foray into the area. From the State Museum of Art return to Elizabetes iela and proceed a little way north away from the park. Quite soon you will come to 10b Elizabetes iela, a highlight among Mikhail Eisenstein's art nouveau buildings. Make sure you cross the road to look up at it or you will miss the impressive details at the top.

At the south end of the Esplandade Park on Brīvības bulvāris is the **Russian Orthodox Cathedral** (page 169 [1 B3]), with its distinctive domes surmounted by Orthodox crosses, built in 1876–84 to designs by Roberts Pflugs. During the Soviet years it was used as a planetarium and for scientific lectures. Now it has been handed back to the Orthodox church, and has been magnificently restored.

Opposite the cathedral, the large government building is the Ministru kabinets, the Cabinet Office.

If you are interested in churches, it is worth continuing up Brīvības iela for two blocks beyond the Hotel Latvija, where you will come to another Russian Orthodox building, the **Alexander Nevsky Church** [1 C2] on the corner of Brīvības iela and Lāčplēša iela. It is named after the 13th-century Russian prince who was canonised by the Russian Orthodox Church in 1547 for his efforts to preserve Orthodoxy in Russia against the Germans whom he defeated at Lake Peipus (now in Estonia) in 1242, a story immortalised in Eisenstein's 1938 film (Sergei Eisenstein, born in Riga and son of Mikhail, whose work is prominent in the art nouveau area of Riga). A little further on, down Ģertrūdes iela on the left of Brīvības iela, is **St Gertrude's Church** [1 C2], a large red-brick church built in 1863–67 to designs by J D Felsko. The plain interior and pleasing woodwork and gallery are typical of so many Latvian churches.

Wander back towards the parks through the boulevards lined with shops and, increasingly, cafés and restaurants, and admire the many different styles of art nouveau buildings on Terbātas iela, Lāčplēša iela and the surrounding streets.

MOSCOW DISTRICT WALK

Depending on how energetic you are feeling, you can either walk to the Maskavas district or take tram number 7 from the stop opposite the National Opera on Aspāzijas bulvāris. Either way, you will start off going round or through the **Central**

Market (*Centrāltirgus* [1 B4]). In the 19th century this area was full of what used to be called 'red warehouses' (some still stand), so called after the colour of the bricks used to build them. The modern market buildings consist of five large pavilions, each one originally designed to deal with a different product. Each one is 12m high and covers an area of 75,000m^2, and was built in 1930 to a design intended for Zeppelin hangars. Apart from the formal market, the area around the hangars is full of stalls selling all manner of food, clothing and other goods. Maskavas iela starts at the end of the market, close to the river. Whether on foot or by tram, follow this road away from central Riga, and very shortly you will see on your left an excellent example of Soviet architecture of the Stalin era in the form of the **Academy of Sciences** building. Built in 1957, its nickname, 'Stalin's birthday cake', reflects its ornateness. Similar buildings can be found in Moscow and Warsaw. Though they are now faded and difficult to see, sharp eyes may spot the Communist hammer and sickle motifs close to the top. A little further on, also on your left, is the **Evangelical Lutheran Church of Jesus**. Strūgu iela (between Gogoļa iela and Maskavas iela, just before the elevated Lāčplēša iela) reflects the area's Russian past: the name means 'Barge Street' and recalls the days when barges and rafts sailed along the Daugava between Riga and ports in Russia.

Before long the road passes under the elevated approach to Salu bridge and you find yourself in **Maskavas District** (Maskavas Forštate), so called because it was a Russian area in earlier times (Maskva = Moscow in Russian) and the road to Moscow passed through it. For many years it was inhabited mainly by Russians and

Jews and, although this is no longer the case, it continues to attract a high proportion of people of non-Latvian origin. The area is a quiet haven where it is easy to imagine yourself back a hundred years: the streets are still cobbled, many of the houses wooden, trees and parks plentiful and the number of cars typically very few.

If you have come by tram, get off at Mazā Kalna iela (two stops after coming under the elevated road). The area near the junction of Maskavas iela and Mazā Kalna iela used to be known as Krasnaja Gorka (Red Hill) and was where the Russian population of Riga came to celebrate the first Sunday after Easter, a traditional Orthodox feast day. The traditional Russian name is barely remembered now, but the tradition remains alive in the name of the nearby street, Sarkanā iela (Red Street). Walk up Mazā Kalna iela as far as you can go, noting the traditional 'shops' on the left (holes in the wall), and you will come to the **Russian Orthodox Church of St John the Baptist** at the edge of the **Ivan Cemetery** (Ivana Kapi). If you are interested in trains, you can turn left when leaving the church and walk along Lielā Kalna iela. Where the road turns you will find a footbridge across a huge swathe of railway lines. From the centre of the bridge is a good view of Riga New Town, including the dominant Reval Hotel Latvija. If trains are of little interest, turn right out of the church and then right along Daugavpils iela. A left turn along Jēkabpils iela leads through two parks, formerly cemeteries, **Klusais dārzs** (Quiet Garden) to the left and **Miera dārzs** (Peace Garden) to the right. Each has a church in its ground: St Francis, a Catholic church in the latter, and All Saints, a

JEWISH RIGA

For information on the Jewish ghetto, see below.

The only **synagogue** that now operates in Riga is in Peitavas iela. The site of what used to be the main synagogue (the **Choral Synagogue**) on the corner of Dzirnavu iela and Gogoļa iela is marked by a memorial (not a very impressive one) consisting of parts of the old synagogue set in a sort of park. A plaque records the destruction of the synagogue on July 4 1941. Number 29 Dzirnavu iela was also the site of a Jewish school until 1940. It opened again in 1989 as the only recognised Jewish school in the country.

There is a **Jewish Museum** and community centre (page 153) at 6 Skolas iela, a short walk from the Reval Hotel Latvijā, which deals with the history of Jewish life in Latvia since the 18th century and the revival of Jewish life in the country since independence.

A number of **plaques** in Riga commemorate influential Jews in Latvia. At 2a

Russian Orthodox church in the former. At the edge of the park turn left down Katoļu iela as far as Maskavas iela.

It was in this area that the **Jewish ghetto** was established in 1941. In August 1941 the Rigan citizens who lived in the district were moved to locations closer to the centre of the city, and by October an area of about 750m² had been formed

Alberta iela a plaque marks the house where Sir Isaiah Berlin, 'the British philosopher', lived between 1909–15. At 6 Blaumaņa iela there is a plaque for Marks Razumnijs (1896–1988), a Jewish poet and playwright.

On Ķīpsala (Kip island) is the **house of Jānis Lipke** (1900–87) who sheltered 53 Riga Jews in his house on the island during World War II. As their number grew, two large cellars were dug to conceal them, and 43 survived the war.

On the outskirts of Riga are also a number of sites which may be of interest. **Rumbala**, 10km outside Riga off Maskavas iela, is a site where some 25,000 Jews from the Riga ghetto were murdered in 1941. **Biķernieku mežs**, also close to Riga, is a similar site. A memorial was recently dedicated to the victims here by the Latvian president. To get there take bus number 14 from Brīvības iela to Biķernieku mežs. Finally, **Salaspils**, 20km south of Riga, was a Nazi camp where many thousands of people, including Jews, were killed (page 221).

taking in Lāčplēša iela, Maskavas iela, Ebreju iela (Jews' Street) and Daugavpils iela. The total Jewish population of the ghetto was about 30,000. The men in the ghetto who were fit to work were put to forced labour; the others were taken to Rumbula Forest on November 30 1941 and systematically murdered by German guards with the assistance of a significant number of Latvian collaborators. Other Jews were brought in to replace those murdered, only to suffer the same fate in the forests of Biķernieki or in Dreiliņi. The total number of people killed in this way has never been finally ascertained, but estimates indicate it to be around 50,000. On November 2 1943 the Riga ghetto was closed following the Warsaw ghetto uprising, and the few remaining inhabitants were shot or transported to concentration camps. No trace of the ghetto remains today, although there is a Jewish cemetery (Ebreju kapi) not far away between Tējas iela and Lauvas iela.

A left turn along Maskavas iela, followed by a right turn into Grebenščikova iela leads to the **Church of the Old Believers** (page 169), the glittering dome of which you can see from a distance. The area beyond the church and close to the river has seen considerable development in recent years. The large Mols shopping centre now stands on the river bank and its buildings dominate the environs. Before crossing to it, you may like to visit the **Armenian Apostolic Church** (at the time of writing being restored) on Kojusalas iela. From in front of the shopping centre you can take a shuttle bus back to the station, close to the Central Market.

LEFT BANK WALK

Pārdaugava is the name for the area on the 'left bank' of the Daugava, the part of Riga that lies on the riverbank opposite the Old Town, where up to a quarter of the city's total population lives. It consists of a number of areas, such as Torņakalns and Āgenskalns, which have long since been swallowed up into Riga but which in places retain something of the atmosphere of small provincial towns. It began to be inhabited only after the building of bridges across the Daugava (an iron bridge in 1871 and a pontoon bridge in 1896). Gradually it grew into an area of about 120km² of industrial and residential development. At present the northern area in particular, close to the approaches to Vanšu bridge (Vanšu tilts), is undergoing a further renaissance, as hotels and offices spring up. Particularly controversial is the Saules Akmens (Sun Stone) high-rise office complex being built on Ķīpsala island, which has been criticised by UNESCO's world cultural heritage committee, among others, for being too tall for its location.

You can approach the area on foot by crossing the Akmens tilts (Stone bridge) from the Old Town. If you prefer, take the number 2, 4 or 5 trams from 11. Novembra krastmala to the second stop after the bridge across the river. After crossing the river you come to Uzvaras bulvāris (Victory Boulevard) and the **Latvian Railway Museum** (page 162). The road leads on to **Uzvaras Parks** (Victory Park, page 186), so called to commemorate the liberation from German occupation, with its huge **Soviet War Memorial** (page 187). If you are interested in the theatre, you could take Bāriņu iela, the right fork through the park after Slokas iela, continue a little way beyond the park until you come to Eduarda Smiļģa iela, where you will find the **Theatre Museum** at number 37–39 (page 165). The smaller **Arkādijas Parks** (Arcadia Park) was created in 1852 by the Prussian consul general, Wehrmann (Vērmans). Next to it, **Mary's Pond** (Māras dīķis) is a popular place of recreation. It derives its name from the mill attached to St Mary's Church which was acquired by the city of Riga in 1573. The pond is probably the old mill pond and is sometimes referred to as Mary's mill pond (Māras sudmalu dīķis).

At the edge of Arkadijas parks is Torņakalns railway station (you can also travel here directly, one stop on the railway from the central station). On June 14 2001 a **Monument to the Victims of Communist Persecution** (page 180) was unveiled, and it caused some considerable controversy. If you continue to walk along the road next to the railway lines away from central Riga, you will come shortly to Torņakalns' **Lutheran Church** (Lutera baznīca). The church was opened in 1891 some years after a local pastor had decided to raise funds for a new church to commemorate the 400th anniversary of Martin Luther's birth in 1483. The architect was Johannes Koch (1850–1915), who also worked on fashionable apartment blocks in the New Town. Just beyond the church Torņakalna iela crosses the railway lines on a viaduct designed in art nouveau style. This was the first concrete construction in Riga: according to contemporary reports, many people were afraid to walk across it.

Close by (cross the viaduct, continue to the end of Torņakalna iela and turn right into Vācieša iela) is a museum which commemorates and was formerly the home of a Latvian writer, the **J Akurātera Memorial Museum** (page 145). Alternatively, turn the other way along Torņakalna iela, walk past the cemetery and right into Vienības gatve. Very shortly, at the corner of Altonavas iela, you will see the **Blok estate** (Bloka muižiņa), a well-preserved example of early 19th-century wooden building. Return to the corner of Torņakalna iela and cross into Satiksmes iela and then left on to Jelgavas iela. The bath house along here has a traditional sauna (under Ls2 per person) and also serves food and *kvass* (a refreshing non-alcoholic drink made from either rye bread or fruit, water, yeast and sugar or honey, popular in summer). From here you can easily make your way back to Torņakalns station for the return journey to central Riga.

MEŽAPARKS WALK

The Mežaparks area in the northeast of Riga lies on Ķīšezers (lake) and includes a park, which houses Riga Zoo as well as the immensely large Lielā Estrāde (large stage), a stadium which can hold up to 20,000 singers and 30,000 spectators and is used for the annual Song Festival. The area also includes a spacious residential sector, which claims to be Europe's first garden city. To visit Mežaparks, take tram number 11 from Kr Barona iela to the Zooloģiskais dārzs (Zoological Park) stop, a trip of around 20 minutes. The route takes you past Meža kapi (cemetery, page 191).

The first houses and streets here were built in Kaiser's Park, as it was then called, in 1902 but the area was gradually extended over the next 30 or so years. In its heyday it included art nouveau, functionalist and art deco family houses, all individually designed and all set in spacious green gardens. Between them, the individual gardens boasted around 100 species of trees and shrubs, many of them rare. The majority of owners were Baltic Germans, most of whom left Latvia from 1939 onwards. Under the Soviet occupation the houses, originally intended for one family, were turned into multi-occupancy dwellings and gradually fell into disrepair due to lack of money. Over the last few years, many of the properties have been restored, although some are still in various stages of neglect, and the area is now once again one of the most sought after areas of real estate in Riga.

The best way to see the area is just to wander along some of the streets to the east of Kokneses prospekts. An interesting circular route would take you from the tram stop along Ezermalas iela, right into E Dārziņa iela, right again into V Olava iela, left down Jāņa Poruka iela, right into Vēlmas iela, left into Sigulda iela, left along Kokneses prospekts, a short detour into Visbijas prospekts, returning again to Kokneses prospekts, left along Pēterupes iela, continuing into Hamburgas iela and finally back along Ezermalas iela to the tram stop.

Some houses which may be of interest include the richly decorated Villa Adele at Hamburgas iela 9, now the residence of the German ambassador; the plain house at Jāņa Poruka iela 14, an attempt to create a distinctly Latvian style of functionalism; Hamburgas iela 25, a decorated art nouveau mansion built on top of what used to be a sand dune; and the mansard roofs, verandas and terraces of houses designed around 1911 by architect Gerhard von Tiesenhausen at 2, 4, 6–8 Visbijas prospekts.

Museums and sightseeing

10

MUSEUMS

Riga has a huge number of museums, most of them of a high standard. They tend to be closed on Mondays and sometimes Tuesdays, so if you have a particular interest you should plan your trip carefully.

The only museums open on Monday are the State Museum of Art, the Motor Museum, the Open Air Enthnographic Museum, 'Jews in Latvia', the Sports Museum and the Museum of the Occupation (in summer only). In general museums open at 10.00 or 11.00 and close at 17.00. In summer, a few of the museums stay open until 19.00, usually on Wednesday or Thursday. These include the State Museum of Art, the Arsenal Museum of Art, the Museum of Decorative and Applied Art, the Museum of Natural History, the History Museum and the Photographic Museum.

Which, if any, museums you visit, obviously depends on your personal interests. The most commonly visited museums include the Open Air Ethnographical Museum, the Museum of the Occupation, the Motor Museum, the State Museum of Art, the Jānis Rozentāls Memorial Museum and the adjacent art nouveau houses, and the Blackheads' House.

Jāna Akurātera Museum 6a O Vāciesa iela, Pārdaugava; tel: 761 9934 (across the Daugava River from the Old Town, see 142) Open 11.00–17.00 Wed–Sat.

The wooden house was the home of Jānis Akurāters (1876–1937), the popular Latvian writer, rifleman and later director of the Radio Service in Riga. Right up to his death, he wrote poetry and novels, his best known being *Kalpa zena vasara* (*The Young Farmhand's Summer*) and *Degosa sala* (*The Burning Island*). The fact that the house was not large meant it was not nationalised under the Soviet occupation, and Akurāters' family continued to live there, with his original furniture and other belongings, until 1987.

Arsenal Museum of Art (Mākslas Muzejs Arsenals) 1 Torņa iela; tel: 721 3695 [2 C2] Open 11.00–17.00; closed Mon May 1 to Oct 1 open until 19.00 on Thu.

The museum has a reserve of 12,500 pictures, sculptures etc by Latvian artists who emigrated after 1945. Exhibitions are held on the ground floor and paintings by children displayed on the first floor.

State Museum of Art (Valsts Mākslas Muzejs) 10a Kr Valdemāra iela; tel: 732 4461 [1 B2] Open: 11.00–17.00 every day except Tue. May 1 to Oct 1 open Thu 11.00–19.00. Admission Ls1.20. Tours in English Ls5.

The museum, built in 1905 by Wilhelm Neumann in German baroque style, houses a collection of 32,000 works of art and is a must for anyone interested in 19th- and early 20th-century Latvian art. Inevitably, there is a great deal of work by Rozentāls (his portrait of the singer Malvine Vignère-Grīnberga painted in the last year of his life is particularly well known). Other names, less well-known outside Latvia, are also of interest: Vilhelms Purvītis (1872–1945) whose Impressionist landscapes depict Latvia's forest and lakes; Jūlijs Feders (1838–1909) who painted a vast and imposing landscape of the Gauja valley north of Riga; and many others. Also of interest may be a portrait of the Russian writer Turgenev (painted in 1869) by A Gruzdins (1825–91), a bust of the Russian composer Mussorgsky by Teodors Zaļnkalns (1876–1928), a portrait of Kārlis Zāle (the designer of the Freedom Monument) by Ludolfs Liberits (1895–1959) painted in 1934 and showing a relaxed Zāle smoking a cigarette, and a picture of the old harbour when it was located closer to the Old Town, by Jānis Roberts Tilbergs (1880–1972). Latvia's best-known woman painter is Alexandra Belcova (1892–1981). Several of her portraits are on show. Art by non-Latvian artists is less prominent, but the museum does have a notable collection of paintings of the Himalayas by the Russian artist and explorer Nicholas Roerich (1874–1947). In addition to the permanent collection, the museum also holds frequent exhibitions of works by more modern or contemporary artists. At the entrance is a small area selling postcards of some of the paintings and greetings cards of Old Riga.

The museum is beautifully located in the Esplanade Park. When leaving have a look at the sculpture of Jānis Rainis, one of Latvia's most famous writers and translators, and admire too the building next door, the Latvian Academy of Art, a fine example of neo-Gothic brickwork.

Aviation Museum Riga airport – to the right of the terminal; tel: 720 7482. Allegedly open 10.00–17.00; closed Sat and Sun, but phone to check before visiting.

The museum is not well known by the general public but has achieved cult status among people interested in the Soviet era. The museum contains Soviet helicopters and planes of various ages, including almost all the models of the Soviet MiGs, which can be viewed in detail when the museum is open, or over the wall if it is closed.

Krisjānis Barons Memorial Museum (Krisjāņa Barona Memoriālais Muzejs) 3–5 Kr Barona iela; tel: 728 4265 [1 C3] Open 11.00–18.00 (closed Mon and Tue). Ls0.40.

The museum is the flat (number 5) occupied by Krisjāņis Barons (1835–1923), the Latvian poet and folklorist who is best remembered as the collector of Latvian oral literature, *dainas*, traditional four-line songs. Fearing that traditional Latvian culture would be lost, Barons travelled around the country collecting songs. He also advertised in newspapers and was sent tens of thousands of examples of dainas which he then catalogued. He began to publish his collections of dainas in 1894 and the project eventually ran to six large volumes containing around one and a half million songs. The museum recreates his life and work through documents and photographs. Information is available in English; examples of folk music and videos can also be purchased.

The Blackheads' House (Melngalvju nams) 7 Rātslaukums; tel: 704 4300 [3 B6]
Open 10.00–17.00 except Mon. Admission Ls1.0.

The Blackheads' House, one of Riga's most important monuments, was restored in 1999. The wonderful façade is one of Riga's highlights, both during the day and when floodlit at night. This magnificent house (really a building made up of two houses connected by an enclosed courtyard), with its Dutch Renaissance façade (1620), dated back to 1334 but was badly damaged in World War II and finally destroyed by the Soviets in 1948. The 'Blackheads', first mentioned in 1413, were an association of unmarried merchants who lived in Riga and Reval (Tallinn). Originally a loose association, they grew to become a powerful force. It is believed that they got their unusual name from their black patron saint, St Maurice. The first floor of the building was used for shops and businesses; the guildhall of the association occupied the second floor; the upper floors were used for storage and warehousing.

The huge step-gable is 28m high and highly decorated with statues of people and animals. The building is topped by a large figure of St George which acts as a weather vane. A statue of Roland stands in front of the building. A popular figure in the Middle Ages, and especially in Germany, the Roland statue was originally erected in 1897 but damaged in World War II. A replica has now been erected.

The interior is now a museum. Particularly impressive is the assembly hall on the first floor. Although none of the paintings here are original, they are faithful copies. Note the Swedish and Russian royal families looking across the floor at

Museums

each other. Much of the silver collection which used to be here is now in Bremen, taken by Baltic Germans who left Riga in the 1930s, and some in St Petersburg, although some families have been helping to rebuild the collection in Riga. You can also visit restored rooms on the ground floor and tour the old foundations in the basement.

Cinema Museum (Rigas Kino Muzejs) Krāslavas 22, tel: 722 0282. Open 12.00–17.00 every day except Mon.

The building, which is in the old Russian working-class district of Riga (Maskaras Forštate), used to house the secret printing press used by the communist newspaper, *Cīņa* ('Battle'). You can still visit the secret passages underneath the building and view the model printing presses.

The Cross-Vaulted Gallery of the Dome (see page 168 [2 B4])

'Dauderi' Latvian Cultural Museum (Latvijas Kultūras Muzejs) 30 Sarkandaugavas iela; tel: 739 2229. Open 11.00–17.00 every day except Mon and Tue. Take tram 9 from the centre north to Aldaris.

This museum is housed in an elegant red-brick house and was built between 1897–98. During the first independence it was the summer residence of the Latvian president, Kārlis Ulmanis, before he was deported. It contains a vast collection of memorabilia related to the recent history of the country brought together by Gaidis Graundiņš, a

Latvian living in Germany. There are also mementoes of Latvia's first period of independence, such as banknotes, stamps, photographs and so on, all collected from Latvian exiles.

Museum of Decorative and Applied Art (Dekoratīvi Lietišķās Mākslas Muzejs) 10–20 Skārņu iela; tel: 722 2235 [3 D7] Open 11.00–17.00 every day except Mon; Wed 11.00–19.00.

The Museum of Decorative and Applied Art opened in 1989 in the restored Jura baznīca (St George's Church) in the Old Town, generally acknowledged as the oldest stone-built religious building surviving in Riga. The exhibition hall still has a church-like feel about it, although it has not been used for church services for almost five hundred years. The exhibits include tapestries, pottery, glasswork and sculpture, and the old churchyard has been transformed into a sculpture garden. The building itself has been very well restored, and is sometimes used for state occasions: in 1998 a summit of European prime ministers was held here.

Museum of Fire-fighting (Ugunsdzēsības Muzejs) 5 Hanzas iela; tel: 733 1334. Open 10.00–16.30 every day except Mon and Tue. Admission L0.20.

This unusual museum is housed in an art nouveau fire station built in 1912 just north of the art nouveau district and contains displays depicting the history of fire-fighting in Riga. The engines displayed go back to 1899 and include a Chevrolet from America. Whatever the nature of the regime, many fire crews in Latvia have been voluntary, and there are photographs of them in action and posing formally. Foreign fires are covered too, from Moscow in 1812 to New York in 2001. A major feature is a fire engine built during the first period of independence.

Latvian Museum of Foreign Art (Latvijas Ārzemju Mākslas Muzejs) 3

Pils laukums; tel: 722 6467 [2 B2] Open 11.00–17.00 every day except Mon. Admission L1.20.

Housed in part of Riga Castle, the museum consists of three floors of paintings, sculptures, drawings and ceramics by artists from Germany, Holland, France and Belgium. It is a rather odd museum: many of the oldest exhibits (sculptures from Greece and Rome and artefacts from ancient Egypt) are mixed up with modern works; the more conventional galleries exhibit paintings by 17th-century Dutch artists, German works dating from the 16th–19th century and Belgian painting of the 20th century. There are almost no works of great distinction.

Latvian History Museum (Latvijas Vēstures Muzejs) 3

Pils laukums; tel: 722 1357 [2 B2] Open 11.00–17.00 every day except Mon and Tue; Thu 11.00–19.00. Admission Ls0.70. Free on Wed.

This museum, part of the castle complex, traces the history of Latvia and Latvian culture from 9000BC to the present. Each room takes a different and unrelated theme. It is good to see a museum in Latvia that is keeping up to date and where care is taken over presentation and lighting. Do not judge the museum by the gloomy entrance to the building or by the torn signs on the stairs. One room concentrates on archaeology but sadly the labels are only in Latvian; another covers religious statues in both stone and wood which have been rescued from churches all over the country. Turning to more modern history, there are models and original tools to display 19th-century farming, a school room from the 1930s and a costume room from the same period. When the EBRD (European Bank for Reconstruction and Development) met in Riga in May 2000, a permanent coin room was set up in the museum. The coins on display go back to the 9th century but of most interest, perhaps, are those from the 1914–20 period when German and Russian ones circulated side by side. A hat exhibition opened in 2002.

'Jews in Latvia' Museum 3rd floor, 6 Skolas iela; tel: 738 3484 [1 B2] Open 12.00–17.00 Sun–Thu. Admission free.

The museum is in the New Town in a street close to the Reval Hotel Latvija. This small but moving museum is devoted to the history of Jews in Latvia, from the first records of Jewish families living with full civil rights in Piltene in the mid-16th century, through growing discrimination in the 19th and early 20th century to the destruction of the synagogues in Riga, Jelgava and Liepāja in 1941 and the terrible sufferings subsequently imposed by both the Nazis and the Soviets. The exhibits, in English as well as Latvian, illustrate the many fields in which Jews contributed to Latvian life in the past, and continue to do so today. On the staircase going up to the museum are photographs and descriptions of some of the Latvians who saved Jews from persecution during World War II, sometimes at the cost of their own lives.

Museum of Riga's History and Navigation (Rigas Vēstures un Kugniecības Muzejs) 4 Palasta iela; tel: 735 66 76; www.vip.lv/museums/riga [2 B5] Open 11.00–17.00; closed Mon and Tue. Admission Ls1.

Founded in 1773, this is the oldest museum in Latvia. It was originally set up to house items from the private collection of Nicolaus von Himsel (1729–64) whose portrait by an unknown artist hangs in the ground-floor exhibition hall. The main permanent exhibition traces the development of Riga from its beginnings to 1940. It does so by reference to maps, plans, pictures and objects of all kinds from the everyday life of the city's inhabitants.

The collection is weak on the medieval period but particularly strong on 1920–40, showing how affluent and diverse life was for a reasonable number of people at that time. The display covers magazines published in several languages, fans, pottery, glasswork and clothes. In 2002 the impressive Colonnade Hall reopened; it was originally built between 1778 and 1783 but was closed for renovation in 1984 and this has only now been completed. Some of the original brickwork can be seen. It houses a large portrait of Peter the Great arriving in Riga in 1710.

The second main permanent exhibition is devoted to the history of navigation from ancient times to the present day. One room is dedicated to the work of Krišjānis Valdemārs (1825–91), a pioneer in naval education in Latvia. What is displayed here would be more than enough work for most people, but Valdemārs was also active as a short-story writer, a newspaper editor and as a constant political campaigner in the National Awakening Movement. The exhibition also includes many models of ships which have been connected with Riga from the 10th century to the present day.

Mentzendorff House (Mencendorfa nams) 18 Grēcinieku iela; tel: 721 2951 [3 C8] Open 10.00–17.00 every day except Mon and Tue. Open by prior arrangement for groups on Mon and Tue. Admission Ls1.20. Guided tours in English Ls3.

The former residence of a wealthy Riga merchant family this house is now a museum devoted to life in Riga in the 17th and 18th centuries. The building dates from the 1720s when it replaced an earlier one destroyed in the Riga fire of 1677. Wall paintings from that time have only recently been discovered; in some rooms there were as many as five layers of paintings and then 20 layers of wallpaper from the 19th and 20th centuries. Some of the early paintings were modelled on the work of the French artist Antoine Watteau (1684–1721). The house now carries the name of the last Baltic German family to live here until 1940, though is sometimes still called the 'Merchant's House' in view of the number of trades carried out here. The outlines of the grocery store that the Mentzendorff family ran can be seen on the ground floor, although not all the articles displayed are originals from this house. Note the raised edge of the long wooden table, which prevented coins slipping to the floor. In winter, the kitchen stove was the centre of the

Museums

household: it was used to cook the food, smoke the meat and heat the whole house. The basement is used for temporary art exhibitions, but the higher floors display furniture, clothes, clocks, playing cards and musical instruments which the Baltic Germans would have enjoyed in the 18th and 19th centuries. In Soviet times 15 different families lived in the building and they were only moved out in 1981 for restoration to begin. It was completed in 1992.

Motor Museum (Rigas Motormuzejs) 6 S Eizenšteina iela; tel: 709 7170. Open 10.00–18.00 Tue–Sun; 10.00–15.00 Mon.

The museum is around 8km from the Old Town. The best way to go by public transport is to take a number 14 trolleybus from Brīvības iela or a number 18 from Čaka iela and get off at Gaiļezers hospital, about 500m from the museum. The museum is not easy to spot: look out for what appears to be a large Audi dealership and showroom; it is a modern red-brick and glass building. The entrance is reached via a bridge from the car park.

The museum houses an acclaimed collection of over 100 motor vehicles, including cars which once belonged to the Soviet leaders, Stalin, Khrushchev and Brezhnev, and Erich Honecker, the leader of the former German Democratic Republic. Wax figures of some of these former politicians and motor enthusiasts help to liven up the displays: Stalin sits in his armoured ZIS 115 (said to have done 2.5km to the litre), Brezhnev at the wheel of his crashed Rolls-Royce, Gorky stands next to his 1934 Lincoln.

The first car assembly plant in Tsarist Russia was established in Riga in 1909 and this was followed by no fewer than 30 bicycle factories during the first independence period. Their products are also exhibited here, as are later Soviet motorbikes. A lot of the cars that form the backbone of the collection were abandoned in 1939–40, firstly by the Baltic Germans recalled 'home' by Hitler, and secondly by the embassies closed after the Soviet occupation. Others are German cars abandoned during the long retreat towards the end of World War II. One is a Rolls-Royce which had been built under licence in Germany. Although the museum is famous for displaying the car that Brezhnev crashed, another one of the 40 or so that he owned is also on display – a 1974 Continental presented by the American government.

Latvian Museum of Natural History (Latvijas Dabas Muzejs) 4 Kr Barona iela; tel: 722 6078 [1 B4] Open: 10.00–17.00 except Mon and Tue; Thu 12.00–19.00. Admission Ls0.60.

The museum has permanent exhibitions of geology, zoology, entomology, anthropology and environmental protection. It also has an exhibition concentrating on the Daugava River and the effect of the construction of the hydro-electric power station on the river basin. Note the herbarium display, the work of the botanist J Ilsters. Most information is in Latvian and Russian only but an interactive computer programme for children on the top floor is in English.

Museums

Museum of the Occupation of Latvia (Okupācijas Muzejs) | Strēlnieku laukums; tel: 721 2715; www.occupationmuseum.lv [3 B7] Open 11.00–18.00. Closed Mon from Oct 1 to May 1. Admission free.

This museum, housed in an exceptionally ugly cuboid building, contains a permanent exhibition devoted to the history of Latvia during the Soviet and Nazi occupations of 1940–91. The displays are on the first floor and exhibit photographs and documents, maps and artefacts dealing with the period and also contain a replica of a barracks room from a Soviet gulag. One display covers the life Latvians led in Siberia after release from the camps but whilst they were still exiled. Another shows the struggle of Latvians in the West to keep the memory of their country alive during the Soviet occupation. Extensive collections of letters, photographs and everyday articles depict the horror of life for those jailed or deported. The renovation of the Hotel Riga provided a new exhibit for the museum – the bugging equipment with which the hotel staff monitored phone calls during the Soviet era. There is excellent background material in English to all the exhibits and a bookshop which sells most of the publications available in English on the two occupations.

The long-term future of the building is a subject of great controversy. Some Latvians feel that the theme of the museum is so important that even if another building were found elsewhere (unlikely under current financial circumstances) it would suggest a loss of interest in the topic on the part of the city administration. Others feel that a Soviet building, whatever its current contents, should no longer be allowed to disfigure the heart of Latvia's capital. The Latvian-born architect Gunars Birkerts, who now practises in America, has suggested alterations to the building which might provide an appropriate compromise and which would certainly make it aesthetically acceptable. No decision has yet been made.

Open Air Ethnographical Museum (Latvijas Etnogrāfiskais Brīvdabas Muzejs) Brīvības gatve 440; tel: 799 4515. Open daily 10.00–17.00. Admission Ls1.

On the northeastern outskirts of the city close to Lake Jugla, about half an hour by bus number 1. Get on at the corner of Merķeļa iela and Terbātas iela and get off at the Brīvdabas Muzejs stop.

Although modern Riga has much in common with other European capitals, a visit to the beautifully constructed Open Air Ethnographical Museum will help you understand some of the more distinctive elements of Latvian history and tradition. It will certainly make you appreciate too how close nature lies to the heart of every Latvian and just how attractive Latvian nature can be.

'Museum' is something of a misnomer for this 100-hectare site, which contains farms, churches, windmills, houses, fishermen's villages and many other buildings, set in a huge pine forest next to Lake Jugla. Brought together from all parts of Latvia, some buildings date back to the 16th century. Most constructions are wooden and blend beautifully with the surrounding trees. It is a pleasure just to walk among them, as well as to learn more about traditional Latvian life from the many exhibits.

Museums

At the weekends it is usually possible to watch craftsmen at work: a blacksmith forging a hunting knife, a woman weaving traditional clothes.

Some favourites are the strange traditional *dore*, hollowed tree-trunks standing on stone bases and used for bee-keeping; wooden *pirts*, traditional baths; the wooden Usma church, which is still used for church services and weddings; and the 18th-century *krogs* (pub) which serves traditional food and drinks including barley beer. You should allow at least two hours for a visit, and you could easily spend a half or even a whole day here.

Latvian People's Front Museum (Latvijas Tautas Frontes Muzejs)
Vecpilsētas 13–15; tel: 722 4502 [3 D9] Open Tue 14.00–19.00, Wed–Fri 12.00–17.00, Sat 12.00–16.00. Admission free.
This is a small, recently opened museum in the former offices of the popular movement which contributed so much to the regaining of Latvian independence. It displays pictures of the movement's leaders and the demonstrations leading up to independence and also shows how the office looked in its period of struggle.

Pharmaceutical Museum (Farmācijas Muzejs) 13–15 Riharda Vāgnera iela;
tel: 721 6828 [3 D7] Open 10.00–16.00 Tue–Sat.
Part of the Paul Stradin Museum of the History of Medicine, this branch is housed in a beautifully renovated 18th-century house in the Old Town. It has an extensive collection of documents, samples of medicine manufactured in Latvia and many

other pharmacy-related items which non-visitors would be hard-pushed to imagine. The interior of a 19th-century chemist's brings it all to life.

Latvian Photographic Museum (Latvijas Foto Muzejs) 8 Mārstaļu iela; tel: 722 7231; www.culture.lv/photomuseum [3 D9] Open 10.00–17.00 Tue, Fri, Sat; 12.00–19.00 Wed and Thu; closed Sun, Mon. Admission Ls1.

The basic exhibition is of cameras and pictures from 1839 to 1941, including many of historic events such as the 1905 Revolution and World War I. A studio from 1900 has also been set up, where it is possible for visitors to take a photo

Pharmaceutical Museum

using the technology of that time. An interesting exhibit is dedicated to the Minox 'spy camera', invented by Walter Zapp, who was born in Riga in 1905 (page 6). The cameras were made in Riga between 1938 and 1943 and have been used ever since. The museum is now gradually being extended to cover World War II.

Rigas Porcelain Museum (Rigas Porcelāna Muzejs) Kalēju 9–11, in Konventa Sēta courtyard; tel: 750 3769 [3 D7] Open 11.00–18.00. Closed Mon. The museum opened to acclaim in 2001 and is the only porcelain museum in the Baltic states. Riga has a long history of making porcelain, starting with the opening of the Kuznetzov factory in the first half of the 19th century, and the 6,000 exhibits reflect the many types of porcelain, from prestigious tea sets to crockery for everyday use, which have been made in the city from the mid-19th century to the present day. One room is devoted to items from the Soviet era, including vases and statues of Lenin, Stalin and other leaders. By far the most dominant item is a 2m-high red and gold vase made to celebrate Riga's 700th anniversary in 1901. Visitors can see demonstrations of porcelain manufacturing and for Ls3 can take part and decorate mugs themselves.

Latvian Railway Museum (Latvijas Dzelzcela Muzejs) 2–4 Uzvaras bulvāris; tel: 583 2849 (just across the river from the Old Town, five minutes beyond the Akmens bridge). Open: 10.00–17.00 Wed–Sat. Admission Ls0.50.

The museum dates from 1994 and is run by Latvian Railways. During its short life it has accumulated a wide range of materials going back about 100 years, including signals, timetables, track and above all, steam engines. One German engine from World War II is fitted out as a snowplough. As late as April 1944, the Germans produced a timetable for the whole Baltics area. It is displayed here and it remains the last one to have appeared. The Soviets regarded such information as too dangerous to impart and the three Baltic railway administrations have been unable to co-ordinate a similar publication. Railway enthusiasts may be interested to know there is another branch of the museum at Jelgava (one hour by bus from Riga), which concentrates on railway safety and training.

Jāņis Rozentāls and Rūdolfs Blaumanis Memorial Museum (Jāņa Rozentāla un Rūdolfa Blaumaņa Memoriālais Muzejs) 12–19 Alberta iela; tel: 733 1641 [1 A1] Open 11.00–18.00 except Mon and Tue. Admission Ls0.60.

The entrance to this museum is on Strēlnieku iela. It commemorates the life and work of two well-known Latvians: Rozentāls, the painter, lived here between 1904 and 1915; Blaumanis only for two years. Take the elaborate staircase in the rather neglected hallway to the top floor and ring to gain admission. The ironwork, the tiling and the paintings on the ceiling are all original but the windows are of a later date. The architect for the building was Konstantīns Pēkšēns (1859–1928). He designed it for his own use, but then gave the top floor to Jāņis Rozentāls in 1904. Rozentāls and his wife Elija, a renowned mezzo-soprano, lived here with their three children. The writer Rūdolfs Blaumanis rented a room in the flat and lived here in 1906–08. The living rooms contain pictures, photographs and artefacts connected with the life of the artists. The studio and other rooms on the top floor are an art school and are used to exhibit works by the students who range from young children to mature painters. Good photographs of Alberta iela can be taken from the top floor.

Latvian Sports Museum (Latvijas Sporta Muzejs) 9 Alksnāja iela; tel: 721 5127 [3 D9] Open 11.00–17.00 Mon–Fri, 11.00–17.00 Sat.

This has a unique collection of bicycles, including a collapsible Peugeot built in 1915 and used during World War I and an English Raleigh lady's bicycle dating from 1895, as well as more conventional exhibits. It is housed in an attractive 17th-century warehouse.

Paul Stradin Museum of the History of Medicine (P Stradiņa Medicīnas Vēstures Muzejs) 1 Antonijas iela; tel: 722 2656; www.mvm.lv [1 A2] Open: 11.00–17.00 every day except Sun and Mon and last Fri of each month.

Located in the New Town on the corner of Antonijas iela and Kalpaka iela. This museum is the creation of the Latvian doctor and surgeon, Paulis Stradiņš, (1896–1958) who collected the majority of the exhibits over a period of 30 years and presented them to the city of Riga. The exhibits, which include medical instruments, books and papers, cover a wide range of topics, from Riga during successive plague epidemics to how the human body copes with eating in space.

Latvian War Museum (Latvijas Kara Muzejs) 20 Smilšu iela (in the Powder Tower); tel: 722 8147; www.karamuzejs.lv [2 D4] Open 10.00–18.00 every day except Mon and Tue. Admission Ls0.50.

During the Soviet occupation this museum was devoted to demonstrating how Latvia became a revolutionary Soviet state. Now it is a mainstream war museum with collections of army uniforms and other exhibits devoted to the military history of Latvia. Exhibits cover the period from the 15th to the 20th century but the main part of the collection focuses on the traumatic events of the 20th century. Of particular interest are the exhibitions devoted to the Latvian Riflemen's

Regiment, and a recent addition, the development of the Latvian army from World War I to 1940.

Theatre Museum (Eduarda Smiļģa Teātra Muzejs) 37/39 Smiļģa iela, in Pārdaugava (page 141); tel: 611893. Open 11.00–18.00 (12.00–19.00 Wed) every day except Mon and Tue.

This museum is housed in the building where theatre director and actor Eduards Smilģis (1886–1966) lived for all but five years of his life. It was empty for five years after his death before being converted into a museum that opened in 1974. Although his personal theatre here could have accommodated an audience, he always rehearsed in strict privacy, totally on his own. This theatre was modelled on the Daile Theatre in central Riga. He played every major role in the plays of Jānis Rainis and of Shakespeare, and when he gave up acting in 1940, he continued to direct. Both his sons were killed fighting, one in the German army and one in the Russian army. The collections comprehensively cover the history of the Latvian theatre, not only in Riga but also in Ventspils and in Liepāja. No famous actor is missed, nor any famous stage-set. The private rooms and offices have been left just as Smilģis would have known and used them.

Museum of Writing, Theatre & Music (Rakstniecības, Teātra un Mūzikas Muzejs) 2 Pils laukums; tel: 721 1956 [2 C2] Open 10.00–17.00 every day except Mon and Tue. Admission Ls0.40.

The fomer Rainis Museum, founded in 1925 and devoted to Latvian literature, has recently been re-branded as the Museum of Writing, Theatre and Music. Permanent exhibits include photographs, manuscripts and texts relating to the history of Latvian literature from its earliest times right up to the 20th century. Recent additions are two exhibitions devoted to Gunārs Freimanis (1927–93) and Voldemārs Zariņš (1917–81), both of whom were persecuted by the Soviet authorities. Freimanis spent ten years in the Russian gulags; Zariņš was sent to forced labour in the coal mines of Tula. Other exhibitions are changed periodically. Unfortunately, all the information (except for a short pamphlet) is in Latvian.

CHURCHES

Churches are one of the highlights of a visit to Riga. Three spires dominate the Old Town skyline, St Peter's, the highest, the Dome and St Jakob's, but other churches are also well worth a visit, including St John's, the Orthodox Cathedral and the Grebenshchikova Church of the Old Believers.

Like museums, several churches close on Mondays and/or at weekends, including the Dome, St John's and St Peter's, so check opening hours when planning your visit.

Dome Cathedral (Doma baznīca) Doma laukums (Dome Square); tel: 721 34 98 [3 C5] Open Tue–Fri 13.00–17.00; Sat 10.00–14.00; closed Sun, Mon. Admission Ls0.50. See note on page 168.

Although size alone does not justify a visit, there is no denying the huge dimensions of this, the largest church in the Baltics. The solid brick walls and 90m tower dominate not only the Cathedral Square but much of the Old Town, and have done so for almost 800 years. Commonly known as the Dome Cathedral (a tautology, as Dome comes from the German *Dom* meaning cathedral), the church was built at the instigation of Albert, Bishop of Riga, now buried in the cathedral. The foundations of the church were laid in 1211 and the building consecrated in 1226. Over the years, the church has been modified and reconstructed a number of times, with the result that it is now a mixture of various styles, although it retains a strong Teutonic flavour.

Originally the church was built on a hill but today visitors walk downhill from Dome Square to enter via the main door. This is because earth has gradually been built up around the cathedral to try and avoid the floods which used to occur frequently in Riga. On one occasion in 1709 it is even reported that fish were caught inside the church.

After it became a Protestant church in the Reformation, much of the cathedral's elaborate interior decoration was destroyed. A striking feature which remains is the large number of coats of arms of merchants from Riga fixed on the sides of the immense pillars, all of which were donated by rich mercantile families in search of immortality. Of interest too are the stained-glass windows. Two towards the front on the north side illustrate important moments in Riga's history: one depicts Walter von Plettenberg reading the edict proclaiming religious freedom and pledging protection

Churches

from the Catholic bishops (1525) and another the welcome of the Swedish king, Gustavus Adolphus, in Riga on September 25 1621. The impressive wooden pulpit, in the middle of the church in accordance with Lutheran tradition, dates from 1641.

What the Dome Cathedral is most famous for, however, is its organ, a huge instrument with four manuals and a pedal board, 124 stops and 6,718 pipes. When it was built in 1884 by the firm of Walcker & Co of Ludwigsburg it was the largest organ in the world.

Note: the cathedral was closed in late 2004 due to a dispute over ownership, but re-opened partially at Christmas 2004 and hopefully will soon re-open fully.

The Cross-Vaulted Gallery of the Dome, the cathedral cloister and courtyard. Next to the main cathedral entrance [2 B4] Open daily in summer 10.00–17.00. Small admission charge.

The cloister itself is a remarkable Romanesque masterpiece, with impressive ornamentation of twining flowers and leaves. Restoration has been in progress since the mid-1980s but is not yet complete. Displayed within the cloister is an assortment of items, including the original weathervane from the Dome spire, a cockerel some 6ft tall, originally constructed in 1595 but replaced by a replica in December 1985; a plaster copy of the statue of Peter I, the original of which stood between 1910 and 1914 where the Freedom Monument now is; and a 3ft-high stone head, unearthed in the cloister in 2000. This last exhibit is still something of a mystery. Originally found in 1851 near Salaspils (just outside Riga), the stone was then lost for almost 150 years. It is possible that the head served as an idol for the Livs, the group of people who have lived on what is now Latvian territory for over 20 centuries. Records exist of the worship and making of idols in Latvia as late as the 16th to 18th centuries, but to date no other idol has been found with such strange and expressive features.

Grebenshchikova Church (Grebenščikova baznīca) Krasta 72 at the end of Grebenščikova iela; tel: 711 3083. Tram 7 or 9 from opposite the National Opera to the Daugavapils stop (approx 10 minutes)
This is a church used by Orthodox Old Believers, a sect which fled from persecution in Russia in the 18th century. Their first church was erected on this site in 1760 but was burnt down and replaced by the current one in 1814. The steeple was added later, in 1906, and has traces of art nouveau in its design. It is surmounted by the only golden dome in Riga and can easily be spotted from any high building in the city centre. The interior contains icons dating back to the 15th century.

Orthodox Cathedral (Pareizticīgo Katedrāle) Brīvības bulvāris, in the Esplanade Park; tel: 721 1216 [1 B3]
The Russian Orthodox Cathedral with its five imposing cupolas offers an insight into another aspect of multi-sided Riga: traditional Russian culture. Built between 1876 and 1884 to designs by Roberts Pflugs, the cathedral was used as a lecture hall and then as a planetarium in Soviet times, and even today Rigans often refer to

Churches

it as the *planetārijs* – the planetarium. It now functions again as a place of worship and has been beautifully restored. The final touches are still being made, and there are plenty of opportunities to donate to the restoration fund. The interior now sparkles with newly gilded coffins, iconostases (screens containing icons) and wall and ceiling paintings. During the Soviet occupation the crosses were removed from the building. Those now in the cathedral were made in Würzburg in Germany, consecrated in 1990 and given to the cathedral by a Latvian living in Germany.

Our Lady of Sorrows (Sāpju Dievmātes baznīca) Lielā pils iela [2 B3]
The Roman Catholic Church of Our Lady of Sorrows dates from 1784–85, although a humbler church was located on the site before the Russian tsar Paul I and the king of Poland, Stanislav August, were persuaded by the Austrian emperor, Joseph II, to donate money for the construction of the present church. For many years it was the only Roman Catholic church in Riga and the surrounding area. The statue of the Sorrowful Virgin above the outside door originally belonged in St. Jacob's Church, but was left there by the Jesuits, later found by the Lutherans and given to this congregation.

St Jacob's or St James' (Jēkaba baznīca) Klostera 2; tel: 732 6419 [2 C3]
Open for visits 07.00–20.00; closed Sat. Note: Jacob and James are alternative translations of the Latvian Jēkabs.

Now the Roman Catholic Cathedral of Riga, the church was originally built in 1225–26. It has subsequently been rebuilt several times, although the sanctuary and the tall, whitewashed brick naves are original. The 73m spire is the lowest of the three spires which dominate the Old Town. The church has changed hands on several occasions: in 1522 it was the first church in Latvia to hold a Lutheran service, but only 60 years later it was handed over to the Jesuits. In 1621 it became a Swedish garrison church before finally returning to the Roman Catholic Church in 1922.

The brick walls have held a number of unexpected items. In 1656 the Russian tsar Alexis Mikhailovich was attacking Riga. During the battle, several grenades hit the church and two of them were later immured above the altar. Then in 1774, during renovation work, the body of a man was found immured in the north wall. His silk garments indicated he was a man of some wealth, but his identity has never been discovered.

St John's (Jāņa baznīca) Jāņa 7; tel: 722 4028 [3 D7] Open Tue–Fri 10.00–17.00.
St John's Church was built for the Dominicans in 1234 but has since been much extended. The stunning high nave with a meshed vaulted ceiling dates from the 15th century and the ornate baroque altar, with sculptures depicting the

Churches

crucifixion and SS Peter and Paul, from the 18th. The altar painting, *The Resurrection*, is by the 18th-century Rigan artist August Stiling, while the painting *Christ on the Cross* in the sacristy is by one of Latvia's best-known artists, Jānis Rozentāls (page 163).

The history of the church again reflects Riga's turbulent past. The Dominicans were ousted in the Reformation, and for some time after 1523 the church was used as stables by the mayor of Riga, then as an arsenal, until in 1582 the Polish king, Stephen Batory, seized it and handed it over to the Jesuits. In due course it was returned to the Lutheran church.

The outside of the church is also worth a good look. Behind the church on Jāṇa iela are two life-sized statues, one of St John the Baptist, the patron saint of the church, and the other of Salome, who persuaded Herodias to give her John's head on a platter as a reward for her dancing. Round the corner, on the wall facing Skārṇu iela, are two stone faces with open mouths. Some sources say they were an early elocution aid – to show monks how to open their mouths to project their voices. Others say they were used to somehow indicate that a sermon was about to begin inside the church. Also on that wall is a covered cross-shaped opening. Legend suggests that in the 15th century two monks voluntarily immured themselves in the wall in the hope of becoming saints. Until their death, passers-by gave them food and water through this hole. Unfortunately their plan did not succeed, as the pope refused to canonise them on the grounds that their motives were callow.

St Peter's Church (Pētera Baznīca) 19 Skārņu iela; tel: 735 6699 [3 C7] Open 10.00–17.00; 10.00–18.00 in summer; closed Mon.

St Peter's tower is the tallest and arguably the most beautiful church tower in Riga. The gracefully tiered steeple rises to a height of 123.5m and, along with the plainer and shorter towers of the Dome Cathedral and St Jacob's, dominates the Old City skyline. If you like bird's-eye views of cities, you can buy a ticket in the church entrance (Ls1.50) and take the lift up to the observation platform.

As you ascend, you may like to consider the tower's rather chequered career. A wooden tower was originally erected in 1491 but collapsed in 1666, killing the inhabitants of a neighbouring building. The replacement tower, completed in 1690, was badly damaged by lightning in 1721 and had to be reconstructed. When reconstruction was completed in 1746, it is said that the builder climbed to the top, drank a goblet of wine and then threw down the goblet: the number of pieces it shattered into would indicate the number of years the building would stand. Unfortunately, the goblet fell into a passing hay cart and suffered only a minor crack, as you can see for yourself if you visit the Museum of History and Navigation. Disaster struck for the third time, ironically on the feast of St Peter (June 29), in 1941 when German mortar fire destroyed both the tower and most of the church. Rebuilding took until 1973. Again a glass was thrown down from the top, but this time it shattered into many pieces. Since then, the only threat to the tower occurred in 2000, when a group of National Bolsheviks from Moscow took over the tower in a bid to reassert Soviet dominance after

Churches

RIGA IN 1992
Frances Samuel

The English Church of St Saviour's, built for the British community in Riga in 1859, had been used in Soviet times as a disco, painted a depressing purple, and was now closed up and empty. A visiting Anglican clergyman, a friend of the then US Ambassador in Riga, offered to hold a communion service in the derelict building. Ten or so of us joined in the first such celebration for 50 years or more, standing in a semicircle in front of a plain wooden table which served as an altar, with a cross made from two wooden poles tied together propped up in a camera tripod, and bread from a local baker's shop. The chalice was an ordinary wineglass we borrowed from the hotel bar. Our vicar had a fine actor's voice, which swept us along as we gave our hesitant

Latvia had regained its independence. Bearing the good omen in mind, visitors can ascend the tower with complete confidence and enjoy a 360° view from the recently renovated observation platform.

The church itself is an excellent example of Gothic architecture. Although first mentioned in records in 1209, only a few sections of the outer walls and some inside pillars remain from the 13th century. The interior style dates mainly from the 15th century, and is impressive in its sheer size and clarity of line. Before 1941 the and emotional responses; it was an extremely moving experience. Some months later a young American Lutheran minister began to hold regular services. The church in those early days was a lifeline for the tiny group of foreign diplomats, traders, students and others, as well as a few brave Latvians, and one splendid old Russian lady. We would gather after a stressful week, stand in a comforting circle for communion and say the Lord's Prayer together, each in her or his own language. Before we left Riga we got a young Latvian silversmith to put a silver collar on the humble wineglass. It is still sometimes used by the now thriving congregation of the fully re-established Anglican church.

Richard and Frances Samuel reopened the British Embassy in Riga in 1991

church housed many religious and art treasures, including a marble pulpit, an oak altar and a magnificent organ. All were destroyed during the war. To commemorate Riga's 800th anniversary, however, seven local students made a reconstruction of the oak altar, based on old photographs, and presented it to the church.

St Saviour's (Anglikāņu baznīca) Anglikāņu iela 21; tel/fax: 722 2259 [2 B3] Open only for services and concerts.

Churches

St Saviour's is Riga's only Anglican church and was built in 1857–59 to serve the English seamen and merchants who came to Riga. The bricks used to build the church were imported from England, as was the layer of soil on which the church was built, although a Riga architect, Johann Felsko, supervised the construction. During Soviet times, the church was used as a discothèque, but was given back to the Church of England when the Archbishop of Canterbury visited Riga in 1994 (see pages 174–5 for a first-hand account of the church in the early days of independence).

BUILDINGS
Guildhalls [2 D5]

At the end of Meistaru iela is what used to be the Guild Square but is now known as the Philharmonic Park (Filharmonijas Parks). The Great Guildhall (Lielā Ģilde) is the large, dull yellow building at one edge of the square, at the corner of Meistaru iela and Amatu iela (Commercial Street). The Small Guildhall (Mazā Ģilde) is right next to it on Amatu iela itself. These buildings represent the centres of Riga's former glory as a Hanseatic City. The Great Guildhall was the council chamber of the merchants; the smaller one housed the council of the less influential craftsmen's guilds. The Great Guildhall was originally established in the 14th century, but has undergone substantial changes over the years. Between 1853–60 it was reconstructed in English Tudor style according to designs by Beine and Scheu. The Old Guild Chamber dates back to the 16th century and is decorated with the emblems of the 45 Hanseatic towns. The so-called 'Brides' Chamber' dates back to 1521: until the 19th century it was still used on the wedding night of children of members of the guild or members themselves. However, a great deal of damage was done by a fire in 1963. Now the building is used as a concert hall. The smaller hall was built (in its present form) between 1864–66. It is also sometimes called the St John's Guildhall – notice the statue of St John with a lamb in one corner of the façade under the tower. Now it is used as offices.

Powder Tower [2 D4]

The Powder Tower (*Pulvertornis*) is one of the oldest buildings in Riga. Its name is derived from the fact that it was once used to store gunpowder, although at times it was also referred to as the Sand Tower after Smilšu iela (Sand Street), the road that leads past the tower and which was once the main road to Pskov in Russia. Records of the tower can be traced back to 1330. The tower is the sole survivor of what used to be 18 towers that formed part of the city fortifications. Because it was used to store gunpowder it had to be dry, well ventilated and secure, hence the walls which are 2$^1/_2$m thick. They were relatively effective: nine cannonballs are said to be embedded in the walls, relics of the Russian invasions of 1656 and 1710. Only the lower parts of the tower are original. The tower was substantially destroyed by Swedish forces in 1621 and restored in 1650.

Since it ceased to have any military significance, the Powder Tower has been put to various uses. In 1892 it was used as the headquarters of a German student

Buildings

fraternity called Rubonia. After World War I it was turned into a war museum. In 1957 it became the Latvian Museum of the Revolution and functioned as such until independence. Now it houses the War Museum (page 164).

Reiter House [3 D8]

The house at number 2 Mārstaļu iela is the Reiter House (Reitera nams), a building that derives its name from another wealthy Riga merchant, Johann von Reiter. The house was built in 1682. Note the six pillars that decorate what appears to be the front of the house but is, in fact, the side. As with the Mentzendorff House, restoration that started around 1980 revealed a large number of wall and ceiling paintings. It is now largely used for lectures and conferences, but the public are able to see the entrance hall and the balustrade leading to the first floor.

Riga Castle [2 B2]

The main building on Pils laukums is Riga Castle (Rigas pils), a large cream building with a red roof. The present structure is the last of three which have stood here. Its predecessors were two Livonian castles, the first of which was built in 1330, the second in 1515. The leader of the Livonian Order lived in Riga Castle up to 1470 when his residence was moved, eventually to Cēsis. The people of Riga destroyed the castle in 1487 but were forced to build a replacement by Walter von Plettenberg, the last head of the Livonian Order. It was completed in 1515 and included the so-called

Lead Tower (*Svina tornis*) which still stands. The castle was extended in the 18th century by the addition of a new wing which became the residence of the Russian governor, and between 1918–40 that of the president of Latvia. It also underwent substantial restoration in 1938 which included construction of the 'three stars tower', easily recognised by the three stars on its top. In the early part of the 19th century Wilhelm von Kester built an observatory on the main tower from which Alexander I of Russia observed the solar eclipse of April 23 1818. Today the castle is once again the residence of the president. It also houses two museums.

The Three Brothers [2 C4]

Returning to Lielā pils iela, turn right into Mazā pils iela, heading away from the tower of Riga Castle. The three houses at numbers 17, 19 and 21 Mazā pils iela are known collectively as 'the three brothers' (*Trīs brāļi*). The oldest is the right-hand house with the Germanic step-gable and dates back to the 15th century. It is claimed that it is the oldest domestic building in Riga. Little is known about its history except that in 1687 it is recorded that it was used as a bakery. Numbers 19 and 21 were built later in the 17th and 18th centuries respectively. In 1966 repair work began with a view to restoring the buildings after years of neglect. Number 17 is set back from the street: when it was built there was less pressure on building land in Riga so a small area was left for stone benches to be installed by the main entrance; but by the time the other houses were built land had become more expensive, so they were built closer to the road and with more storeys so as to maximise land use.

MONUMENTS AND STATUES

Riflemen's Memorial (Strēlnieku piemineklis) [3 B7]

The Memorial to the Latvian Riflemen was erected in 1971 to commemorate the valour of the Latvian Rifle Regiment during the civil war. The Riflemen were first known for their courage in fighting on the front near Riga in 1915. Some of the Riflemen also formed Lenin's bodyguard during the 1917 revolution. During 1917 the Riflemen split into white and red divisions and were caught up on different sides in the struggles of 1918–19: some reds later re-joined the whites and fought against the Germans, but a Latvian Rifleman became the first commander of the Red Army and some reds stayed in Russia and were eventually shot on Stalin's orders in the purges of 1937–38. The statue has long been a subject of strong disagreement. Some see it as an acknowledgement of the bravery of Latvians at the beginning of the civil war, 'a monument to the beginning of the Latvian nation'. Others feel it is too closely allied to the Soviet era and would like it removed and replaced by something more politically neutral.

Monument to the Repressed (Represēto piemineklis)

The work of Latvian sculptor Pēteris Jaunzems and the architect Juris Poga, this monument was unveiled on June 14 2001 to commemorate the 60th anniversary of one of the largest deportations of Latvians to Siberia. In 1941, over 14,000 Latvians were rounded up and loaded into trains at stations around Latvia, including Torņakalns. Families were split up. Women and children were mainly sent to camps in Siberia, men as slave labour to coal mines in the Arctic Circle or uranium mines in Turkmenistan. The modern monument, which has received criticism as well as praise, stands just outside Torņakalns railway station, south of Uzvaras Park, and can be reached by taking a train heading for Jūrmala or Jelgava from the central station; Torņakalns is the first stop (see also page 142).

Statue of Kārlis Padegs [1 B3]

As you walk along Merķeļa iela opposite the House of the Riga Latvian Society, have a look at the artist who will be lolling stylishly against a railing, most probably adorned by flowers from his admirers. The work of Andris Vārpa, this delightfully informal statue, unusual in Riga, commemorates Kārlis Padegs (born in 1911 and died in 1940 in Riga), an idiosyncratic personality in Riga in the 1930s. Padegs broke with the traditional themes of Latvian painting of his time, preferring instead shocking topics, freely expressed. His anti-war paintings and frequently ironic approach were frowned on during the Soviet occupation and his work was rarely seen. The monument was presented as a gift in 1998 by Rita Červenaka-Virkavs, a Latvian artist living in Germany. It has been erected on the spot where Padegs once held an open-air exhibition of his works. (See pages 131 and 134.)

Freedom Monument (Brīvības piemineklis) [1 B3]

The Freedom Monument dominates the centre of Riga. Known locally as 'Milda', it was erected in 1935 and paid for by public subscription. It stands over 350m and is

RIGA'S COAT OF ARMS

Over the centuries Riga has had a number of coats of arms. The present one dates from 1925. The main element, which has existed with variations for many centuries, consists of two towers on either side of an open gate. A golden lion's head stares out from beneath the raised grate of the gate. The whole image symbolises the city's right to autonomy. Above the gate are two crossed black keys, symbolising the patronage of the pope, and a golden cross and crown, symbolising subservience to the bishop. In the current full coat of arms, a shield with these elements is held by two golden lions.

the tallest monument of its kind in Europe. It was designed by the Latvian architect Kārlis Zāle and consists of a tall granite column surmounted by a 9m-high figure of a woman holding three golden stars above her head. The three stars represent the three cultural regions of Latvia – Kurzeme, Vidzeme and Latgale. Engraved in gold letters on the base are the words '*Tevzēmei un brīvībai*' ('for fatherland and freedom'). Also decorating the monument is a sculpture of Lāčplēsis, the legendary Latvian bear-slayer, who has long been a symbol of freedom in the country. The monument was dedicated on November 18 1935, the 17th anniversary of the declaration of independence.

Nowadays the base is often surrounded by flowers, frequently red and white, the colours of the Latvian national flag. Flowers were forbidden during the Soviet era; indeed the Soviet authorities had contemplated removing the monument altogether, since it served as a focus of Latvian nationalistic aspirations, but thought better of the idea, fearing demonstrations and reprisals. Instead they erected a statue of Lenin. The two monuments stood back to back for decades, Lenin facing east towards Moscow, the Freedom Monument facing west. Lenin has now disappeared, but the Freedom Monument remains. The guards who now stand at the monument change every hour on the hour between 9.00 and 18.00.

Monument to the 1905 Demonstrators

In the 1905 park in Grīziņkalns, northeast of the New Town, is a monument to commemorate the meeting place of the 1905 demonstrators (see page 6). It was erected there in 1975 in a park which also includes a stage for musical shows built in 1911. Trolleybus 13 takes you to Pērnavas iela in front of the park.

Statue of Roland [3 B6]

Statues of the knight Roland appeared in Hanseatic towns during the 14th and 15th centuries. Erected as symbols of liberty and independence, they were normally displayed prominently in the main square. Riga was no exception: a wooden statue was made and frequently used as a target during jousting matches and tournaments. Not surprisingly, the wooden statue was frequently damaged and then repaired, so in 1896 a stone statue, designed by Wilhelm Neumann and August Volz, replaced it. The knight rests his left hand on a shield bearing the coat of arms of Riga (see page 182), while in his right hand he holds a sword. It was from the point of this sword that distances from Riga to other places in Latvia were traditionally measured. The statue was damaged in World War II and for many years was not seen in Riga. The original can now be seen in St Peter's Church, while a replica has been placed in the Town Hall Square outside the Blackheads' House.

PARKS AND GARDENS

One of the most attractive aspects of Riga is the large amount of green space in the centre. Almost the whole of the area separating the Old Town and the New Town consists of well-tended parks and gardens which are a delight to stroll through whatever the season. In Riga as a whole, parks make up 19% of the total city area, and lake, rivers and canals a further 16%.

Bastejkalns Park [1 A3]

The parks on either side of the Freedom Monument were laid out in 1853–63. The one through which Brīvības bulvāris runs is the Bastejkalns Park, named after the 17th-century bastion that once stood here and formed a vital part of Riga's defences. If you walk through Bastejkalns Park you will come across a set of engraved stones near the bridge that crosses the canal (most are on the New Town side, one is on the Old Town side of the canal). On the night of January 20 1991 Black Beret forces loyal to Moscow attempted to capture a number of government buildings including the Ministry of the Interior on Raiņa bulvāris, the street running alongside the canal on the New Town side. Several Latvians were shot, some say by sniper fire from the roof tops. The stones preserve the memory of five victims: Gvīdo Zvaigne, a cameraman who was filming events; Andris Slapiņš, a cinema director and cameraman; two militiamen, Sergejs Kononenko and Vladimirs Gomanovics; and Edijs Riekstiņš, a student.

The park also contains monuments to the composer Alfrēds Kalniņš, and the researcher Keldys.

Kronvalda Park [1 A2]

Next to Bastejkalns Park is Kronvalda Park with its monuments to the Latvian writers Edžus and Upīts. Also set in this park are the Riga Congress House (Rīgas kongresu nams) and a monument to Rūdolfs Blaumanis. A canal runs all the way through Kronvalda Park and behind the National Opera, extending in total for 3km,

Parks and gardens

both starting and finishing in the Daugava, thus ensuring a steady flow of water. In summer a popular pastime is hiring pedal boats and drifting along the canal.

Vērmanes Gardens [1 B3]

Bounded by Elizabetes iela Kr Barona, Merķeļa and Tērbates iela, the Vērmanes dārzs (as the gardens are called in Latvian) is the most popular of Riga's central parks. Opened in 1817, it was named in honour of the woman who donated the land to the city. Originally it was a refuge for residents of Riga who could not get out to the countryside. It soon acquired attractions, including a bronze fountain cast in Berlin, a playground, an ice rink, a sun dial and the first rose garden in Riga. It has an open-air theatre and a statue of Krišjānis Barons, the writer and poet.

Uzvaras Park

Walk across Akmens bridge (Akmens tilts) or take the number 2, 4 or 5 trams from 11. Novembra krastmala to the second stop after the bridge across the river. Uzvaras bulvāris (Victory Boulevard), which leads on from the bridge, heads directly to Uzvaras Parks (Victory Park), the largest park in Riga. The plan for the park was made by Georg Kuphaldt in 1909 and, to commemorate 200 years since the incorporation of Riga into the Russian Empire, the park was called after Tsar Peter I. In 1915, while the park was still being completed, Kuphaldt, a German, was expelled from the country along with all his compatriots. A few years later, in 1923, the park was renamed Victory Park (Uzvaras Parks) to commemorate Latvia's liberation from

German occupation – somewhat ironically given the fact that the park was so much the work of a German. Today the park is dominated by the Soviet War Memorial, more correctly the monument to the Fallen Soldiers of the Army of the USSR, Liberators of Riga, and the Latvian SSR from the German Fascist Conquerors. Erected in 1985, the monument was paid for by contributions automatically deducted from the pay packets of workers in Riga. Since the restoration of independence, the monument has become something of a rallying point for communists who meet here on former Soviet holidays. In 1996 some men from an extreme right-wing group tried to retaliate by blowing up the monument but succeeded only in killing themselves.

Arcadia Park

The smaller Arkādijas Parks (Arcadia Park), which directly adjoins it to the south, was created in 1852 by the Prussian consul general, Wehrmann (Vērmans), and acquired by the city in 1896. Next to it, Māras dīķis (Mary's Pond) is a popular place of recreation. It derives its name from the mill attached to St Mary's Church which was acquired by the city of Riga in 1573. The pond is probably the old mill-pond and is sometimes referred to as Mary's mill-pond (Māras sudmalu dīķis).

Riga National Zoo

Meža prospekts 1; tel: 751 8669. Open every day 10.00–18.00. Take tram number 11 from Barona iela to the Zooloģiskais dārzs (Zoological Park); takes around 20 minutes.

Parks and gardens

The zoo, the Baltics' oldest and largest though by no means one of the world's largest, has expanded and improved greatly in recent years and makes a pleasant visit, particularly on a summer day. It is set in the pine forest of the Mežaparks, close to the Ķīšezers lake and next to the Mežaparks garden city. Allow at least two hours to see some of the almost 500 species and over 3,000 animals. Attractions include elephants, camels, bears and ostriches. There are pony rides and other entertainment for children too.

Song Festival Park (Viestura dārzs)

North of the Old Town, on the corner of Eksporta iela and Hanzas iela

This was once a much larger park owned by Tsar Peter I and containing plants brought from all parts of Europe. Although it has been remodelled since then, it is a scenic and well-maintained park with the attraction of being well off the beaten track. It has a playground for children and also a decorative feature to commemorate the centenary of the First Latvian Song Festival which was held here in 1873. The memorial consists of several fountains, a wall with portraits of seven Latvian composers and a large memorial stone. The annual song festival is no longer held here, but in the large open-air auditorium in the Mežaparks (the Mežaparka estrade).

CEMETERIES

Riga has a number of cemeteries that are worth visiting, if time permits, since they reflect something of the history of Latvia and present a number of architectural styles. Three (the Brothers' Cemetery, Rainis Cemetery and Woodlands Cemetery) are close together in an area directly south of Mežaparks. Another two are next to each other, in the same direction but closer to the town centre (the Great Cemetery and Pokrov Cemetery). All can be reached by taking tram number 11 from Barona iela towards Mežaparks. For the Brothers' Cemetery, Rainis Cemetery and Woodland Cemetery alight at the Brāļu Kapi stop. For the Great Cemetery get off at Kazarmu iela. For Pokrov Cemetery alight at the Mēness stop.

The Brothers' Cemetery (Brāfu Kapi)

The Brothers' Cemetery or Cemetery of Heroes is on Aizsaules iela.
The Cemetery of Heroes is a fascinating ensemble of architecture and sculpture in attractive natural surroundings. It was planned in 1915 when thousands of Latvians were dying in the fight against the Germans in Kurzeme, and the same year the first fallen soldiers were buried here. It took 12 years to complete the cemetery, the overwhelming part of the work being done between 1924 and 1936. There are approximately 2,000 graves in Brāļu Kapi, 300 of them simply marked 'nezinams' ('unknown'). On March 25 1988 a memorial service for the victims of the years of the Stalin terror was held here, organised by the Latvian Writers' Association, and 10,000 people attended.

In Latvian folklore the oak symbolises masculine strength, while the lime tree symbolises feminine love; both of these powerful symbols are used extensively in the cemetery. The Latvian coat of arms appears over the entrance gate, while on

Cemeteries

both sides there are sculptured groups of cavalrymen. An avenue of lime trees leads to the main terrace. In the centre an eternal flame burns, flanked by oak trees. Beyond it is the cemetery itself, bordered by trees, shrubs, bushes and walls decorated with the coats of arms of all the Latvian regions and towns.

Especially moving are the Levainotais Jatnieks ('The Wounded Horseman') and Divi brāļi ('Two Brothers') sculptures. At one end of the cemetery stands the figure of Māte Latvijā ('Mother Latvia') who looks down in sorrow at her dead, a wreath to honour her fallen sons in one hand, in the other the national flag. The sculptures are the work of Kārlis Zāle who is himself buried here.

The cemetery was allowed to fall into neglect during the Soviet period, but was restored in 1993 and has since then become a focus of Latvian national feeling.

Rainis Cemetery (Raiņa Kapi)

Aizsaules iela. Latvia's best-loved writer, Jānis Rainis, died on September 12 1929 and was buried here three days later. The cemetery was renamed in his honour. An avenue of silver birch leads to his grave which is marked by a red granite sculpture. Around the monument there is a semi-circular colonnade entwined with ivy.

Alongside Rainis lies his wife, the poet Aspāzija (Elza Rozenberg who died in 1943). The cemetery is also the resting place for a great number of Latvian writers, artists and musicians, many of whose graves are decorated with a creativity to match the lives they were designed to commemorate.

Museums and sightseeing

Woodlands Cemetery (Meža Kapi)

Also on Aizsaules iela, the Woodlands Cemetery was designed by G Kuphalst, the director of Riga's parks, in 1913. Numerous political and government figures from the period of Latvia's first independence are buried here, including the former president, Jānis Čakste, and the government ministers, Zigfrids Meierovics and Vilhelms Munters. In addition, a number of Latvian artists, writers, poets and scientists lie here, among them Jānis Rozentāls, Anna Brigadere and Paul Stradin. In April 1988 Latvia's leading human rights activist, Gunārs Astra, was buried here. Astra was sentenced to seven years' imprisonment followed by five years' internal exile by the Soviet regime in December 1983 for the crimes of possessing recordings of radio programmes, photo negatives and subversive books and for writing a manuscript of a personal nature. In his final words to the court he delivered an impassioned speech against the Soviet regime including these words: 'I fervently believe that these nightmare times will end one day. This belief gives me the strength to stand before you. Our people have suffered a great deal but have learned to survive. They will outlive this dark period in their history.'

The Great Cemetery (Lielie Kapi)

Miera and Senču iela. The cemetery has lost much of its former glory, many monuments having been removed or badly vandalised in the Soviet era and also in the early 1990s, but it still contains the graves of many of Latvia's best-known citizens, including artists, politicians, scientists and business people. Near the

Cemeteries

entrance near Klusā iela is the Green Chapel, the oldest building in the cemetery (1776). Confusingly, it is now a red-brick building, although originally it was a wooden construction painted green and the name has stuck. Graves which may be of interest include a monument to Andrejs Pumpurs (1841–1902), author of the *Lāčplēsis*, the epic poem of Latvia's hero bear-slayer, a large granite pyramid to Patrick Cumming, a Scot who came to Riga in 1777 and later became president of the Riga Stock Exchange; the graves of Krisjānis Barons and Krisjānis Valdemārs; and a memorial, erected in 2001 as part of Riga's 800 years' anniversary celebrations, to the Scot who was mayor of Riga from 1901 to 1912, George Armisted.

Pokrov Cemetery (Pokrova Kapi)

Mēness, Miera and Senču iela. Across the road from the Great Cemetery, this Russian cemetery is in even greater need of care and attention. Many of the gravestones are from the 19th century and commemorate Russians who died in Riga while working for the tsarist government. There is also a large monument dedicated to communist soldiers who fell during and after World War II.

Beyond the City

11

If you are only in Riga for two days, you probably will not want to leave the city itself unless you have a particular interest in other parts of Latvia. If you are there for three days or longer, however, you may well like to take one or more half-day trips, enjoy some of the other attractions of Latvia and gain a broader perspective of the country. Latvia is a small country: everywhere can be reached within a few hours, so in a sense the whole of Latvia is your oyster. The most obvious choices, depending on your interests, are Jūrmala (the seaside area close to Riga), Rundāle (a beautifully restored 18th-century palace close to the Lithuanian border), Cēsis and/or Sigulda (small, historic towns northeast of Riga). A visit to the memorial site of the Salaspils concentration camp is also possible.

JŪRMALA

Jūrmala is not really a place at all but a name: Jūrmala is the Latvian for 'seaside' or 'by the sea' and is in reality the collective name given to a number of small towns and villages along the Baltic coast about 25km from Riga. The beautiful 30-odd kilometre stretch of beach is virtually unspoilt and is the major attraction of Jūrmala. The Gulf waters are clean enough to swim in (the EU blue flag was awarded in 2000), though not always warm enough, and the beaches and woods are ideal for long walks. Sometimes pieces of amber are washed up on the beach, particularly after a storm. Eating and drinking possibilities are good, and if you don't feel healthy enough to enjoy all this, many of the hotels offer spa treatments and massages. Only one word of warning: in hot weather there are often mosquitoes (see *Health* section).

The Jūrmala area first became popular in the late 18th and early 19th centuries, when families began to leave Riga for the summer in search of fresh sea air. Wooden summer-houses quickly began to appear just behind the coastline. The first hotel in the area was built in 1834 in Dubulti; in 1870 the first sanatorium (the Marienbāde in Majori) was constructed; and in 1877 the railway line to Tukums was completed, opening the area up to greater numbers than ever. Mixed bathing was permitted in 1881. The sea air, mild climate, spa water and medicinal mud also made the small, growing towns along the coast a favourite with convalescents, so Jūrmala also gained a reputation as a health resort. The resort was developed even further under the Soviet occupation: hotels, convalescent homes, sanatoria and pioneer camps were built from 1945 onwards, transforming Jūrmala into one of the most important holiday resorts in the Soviet Union, attracting over 250,000 visitors a year. Since the restoration of independence, much work has been done to redecorate the many summer houses that give the town its distinctive feel. In 1997 the government declared the area around Ķemeri, at the far end of Jūrmala, to be a national park. The most popular spots are Lielupe (named after the river which in turn means 'big river'), Dzintari ('pieces of amber') and Majori.

Transport

You can get to Jūrmala from Riga by train, bus, taxi or car. On summer weekends it can also be reached by boat.

Frequent trains depart from platforms 3 and 4 of the central railway station in Riga. It takes about 20 minutes from Riga to the first stop at Lielupe, although not all trains stop there. However, all trains do stop at Majori (about 40 minutes from Riga). Trains are most frequent between May and October (one every 10–20 minutes) and run from about 05.00–23.00. The price is Ls0.20 each way. Note that there is no one station called Jūrmala – it is probably best (unless you have a specific goal) to get out at Majori.

During the summer there are frequent buses from the bus station. Taxis leave Riga from a special taxi rank just outside the station. There is also a comfortable minibus connection between Jūrmala and Riga, running every 20–30 minutes.

Jūrmala is only a 20–30-minute drive from Riga. However, as you approach Jūrmala you must pull into the lay-by at the toll point and buy a special ticket to gain access to the area by car. Tickets cost Ls1 a day.

The boat trip takes two hours and costs Ls3 one way for adults and Ls1 one way for children between 6 and 12 years old. On Saturdays and Sundays in summer the 'Jūrmala' leaves from 11. Novembra krastmala, just next to Vanšu bridge, at 11.00, arriving in Jūrmala at 13.00. The return trip leaves Majori at 17.00, arriving in Riga two hours later. For further information, tel: 957 8329; fax: 734 6515.

Tourist information

Jūrmala Spa and Tourist Information Centre (Jūrmalas Kurorta un Tūrisma Informācijas Centrs) (42 Jomas iela, Majori, Jūrmala, LV-2015; tel: 776 4276/776 2167; fax: 776 4672; email: jurmalainfo@mail.bkc.lv) produces an excellent brochure with up-to-date details of hotels including prices. You should also consult this office for guided tours, information about healthcare and medical facilities in Jūrmala, and hotel reservations.

Accommodation

Jūrmala has a wide selection of medium-priced hotels, and new ones are constantly opening. In the summer season, booking in advance is advisable. We give here only a small selection.

Alve 88a Jomas iela, Majori; tel: 775 5951; fax: 775 5972; email: alve@navigator.lv; www.alve.times.lv

A stylish hotel, with lots of wood and glass, and ten spacious and airy rooms, on the main street in Majori. Spa programmes, including detoxification and relaxation, are offered, with a steam bath, spa bath, thalassotherapy and body wraps available in the spa centre. Convenient location, but can be noisy on summer weekends. Double rooms from Ls45.

Camping Nemo 1 Altbalss iela, Vaiveri; tel: 773 2350; fax: 773 2349; email: nemo@nemo.lv; www.nemo.lv

Spaces for tents and caravans at the Nemo Water Amusement Park, right next to the beach in Vaivari. Open in summer only (May to Sep). Double Ls8–10.

Eiropa (Europe) Hotel 56 Jūras iela, Majori; tel: 776 2211; fax: 776 2299; email: hoteljuras@apollo.lv; www.hoteljuras.lv

Opened in 2004, an elegantly restored art nouveau house with 19 rooms, including some suites. Some 50m from the beach in Majori. Prices include not only breakfast, but also use of the sauna and fitness room. Double rooms from Ls70.

Kurši Guesthouse 30 Dubultu prospekts, Dubulti; tel: 777 1606; fax: 777 1605; email: kursi@angstceltne.lv. Offers self-catering apartments, mostly on two floors, and all with a private shower, toilet, kitchenette and satellite TV, for Ls35–66 a day. For long stays there are substantial discounts, and if you fancy a 'romantic weekend' package, the guesthouse offers a special deal with a candlelight dinner and use of a sauna.

Lielupe Hotel 64–68 Bulduru prospekts, Bulduri; tel: 775 2755; fax: 775 2694; email:lielupe@lielupe.lv

A concrete-block hotel 500m from Bulduri station and 200m from the beach. At the time of writing only half the rooms have been modernised with private bathroom, satellite TV and phone, so if you would like to stay here make sure you have one of these. The advantages of the hotel are the many facilities on hand, including a concert/film hall seating 300, indoor and outdoor swimming pools, indoor and outdoor tennis courts, sauna and massage, fitness studio and solarium; you can also organise horseriding. Double rooms cost from Ls63 a night.

Majori 29 Jomas iela, Majori; tel: 776 1380; fax: 776 1394; email: vmajori@mail.bkc.lv
Recently refurbished, this is one of the better hotels in the area. The art nouveau building, with a green roof and tower, is in the centre of Majori about 250m from the sea. Do not confuse the hotel with the much smaller boarding house of the same name on Smilšu iela. The hotel rooms are pleasantly decorated and all have private bathrooms, a telephone and cable TV. Double rooms cost Ls48–63.

Pegasa Pils 60 Jūras iela, Majori; tel: 776 1149; fax: 776 1169, www.pegasapils.lv
A beautifully restored art nouveau mansion, originally built in 1900, and now offering double rooms and suites with balconies 50m from the beach in Majori and very close to the Dzintari Concert Hall. All the rooms are comfortably furnished and are equipped with AC, a minibar, telephone and satellite TV. The hotel also has a restaurant, sometimes with live music. Double rooms from Ls75.

Youth Hostel of the Latvian University Fund (Jauniešu viesnīca) 52/54 Dzintaru prospekts, Dzintari; tel: 775 1873; fax: 722 8661; email: luf@latnet.lv
20 double rooms with shared showers, toilets and kitchen. Double rooms Ls12.

Eating and drinking

By far the widest choice for eating is along Jomas iela in Majori, where you can find everything from pizza to high-class fish dishes. The best plan is just to stroll along the street and see what takes your fancy. In the unlikely event that nothing does, there are some excellent hotel restaurants too, which are happy to serve non-residents. In summer, most restaurants are open from 12.00 to 23.00, although a few, including Al Tohme, Orients and Coco Loco, claim to stay open until the last guest leaves. If you're visiting in winter, note that most restaurants are open only for lunch. Prices in general tend to be slightly lower in Jūrmala than in Riga: expect to pay between Ls4–6 for a main course in most restaurants. All the restaurants listed here accept credit cards.

Al Tohme 2 Pilsoņu iela, Majori; tel/fax: 775 5755
A rare find, not only because the restaurant is right next to the beach and has views of the Gulf of Riga, but also because it is Lebanese and serves Middle Eastern food. You can also enjoy a narguile (water pipe) as you relax in the stone-mosaic-decorated interior.

Coco Loco Jomas iela 37, Majori; tel: 776 1464
A mixture of Jamaican and European food in a relaxed atmosphere, just off Jomas iela. Never without music.

Il Patio, **Planeta Sushi** 2 Dzintaru prospects, Dzintari
After their success in Riga, these two restaurants, owned by the same Russian company, have now opened in Jūrmala. Unusually you can order from both menus, starting with sushi and finishing with an Italian ice cream.

Kūriņš 47 Kauguciema iela, Kauguri; tel: 773 6598
The restaurant is in a wooden building, in the style of a traditional Latvian fisherman's house, and is located directly on the beach at Kauguri. It offers Latvian specialities, as well as

mainstream European dishes. In summer there is traditional Latvian country music from 22.00 on Fri until early in the morning.

Orients 33 Jomas iela, Majori; tel: 776 2082
Specialises in Russian and Caucasian meat dishes but also serves seafood and oriental dishes. A lively place with exuberant interior décor and live music in the evenings.

Pegasa Pils 60 Jūras iela, Majori; tel: 776 1169
In the newly restored art nouveau hotel Pegasa Pils, this restaurant is classy in atmosphere and in quality of food. The dishes are international and the service excellent.

Salmu Krogs 70/72 Jomas iela, Majori; tel: 776 1393
A large restaurant with a wide choice of grilled fish and meat. A popular place on summer evenings, partly due to its prices, which are lower than many in Jūrmala.

Senators 55 Jomas iela, Majori, tel: 781 1161
A restaurant and bar, with interior and exterior seating, next to the Slāvu Restorans. Enjoy pizza, ice-cream or beer in pleasant surroundings.

Slāvu Restorāns 57 Jomas iela, tel: 776 1401
You won't miss this large restaurant halfway along the main street in Majori. There is seating both indoors and on the terrace and a wide choice of dishes, including many Russian specialities such as caviar and dumplings. Prices are reasonable, at around Ls4.70 for a main course and Ls1.50 for desserts.

Spotikačs 77 Jomas iela, Majori

A restaurant which specialises in Ukrainian food and drink – and if you thought you didn't know what that is, it includes well-known dishes such as chicken Kiev and drinks such as fruit-flavoured vodka. You can sit outside, or in an attractive wooden building with painted bird and flower motifs on the walls. Also in Riga (page 80).

Sue's Asia 74 Jomas iela, Majori; tel: 775 5900

An extensive choice of Indian, Chinese and Thai dishes in an exotically oriental setting. Also in Riga (page 80).

Villa Joma 88a Jomas iela; tel: 775 5971

This green wooden building with an unusual interior décor is the restaurant of the Hotel Villa Joma but is extensively patronised by non-residents. The menu has a wide range of international dishes, including attractions such as duck with caramelised apple and orange sauce, and enticing desserts such as wild berry pie with ice-cream and berry sauce.

Activities

Most people go to Jūrmala to enjoy the beaches or walk in the dunes and forests. The beaches near Majori and Dubulti tend to get very crowded in the short summer season. If you prefer quieter beaches, try Lielupe, at the Riga end of Jūrmala. If you'd like to be more active, you can hire a bike, play tennis, go riding, learn to windsurf or kitesurf, visit churches and museums, or spend some time looking for birds in a national park.

Jūrmala

Bicycle hire

ABS Nomas Grupa Ltd 24 Jūras iela, Majori; mobile: 6 133334; email: velo_abc@one.lv

Bicycle and Tourist Equipment Rental 100 Dubultu prospekts, Jaundubulti; tel: 776 7464

Rental 21 Mellužu prospekts, Melluži; tel: 776 7899. Roller-skates also for hire.

Sports

Bowling At the Bowling Club Rio-Rio inside the 'Grateka' sports and recreation centre, 49 Meža prospekts, Bulduri, tel: 775 4481; email: fitlains@delfi.lv; www.grateka.lv.

Horseriding Try the Riders' Club 'Cavalcade', Horse Riding Therapy Centre, 61 Asaru prospekts, Vaivari, tel: 776 6151; mobile: 9 415916. Horses can also be hired via the Neptuns restaurant (1 Kolkas iela, Jaunķemeri; tel: 773 7951).

Swimming Nemo Water Amusement Park 1 Atbalss iela, Vaivari; tel: 773 2350; fax: 773 2349; email: nemo@nemo.lv; www.nemo.lv. Swimming pools, water slides and saunas. Admission Ls2.50. Open 10.00–22.00 daily in summer.

Tennis At lots of hotels and also at the Sports Centre 'Concept' 36 Vienības prospekts, Bulduri; tel: 714 9911.

Windsurfing and kitesurfing Equipment rental and training available at Burusports 1 Piejūras iela, Pumpuri (at the beginning of Upes iela); tel: 920 7123; email: windguru@kite.lv. Open daily from Jun 1 to Aug 31, 10.00–20.00.

Museums, churches and buildings

The most popular museum in Jūrmala is probably the **Rainis and Aspāzijas Memorial Summer House** (tel: 776 4295) in Majori. It was here that the writer, Jānis Rainis (1865–1929), had his summer house (at 5–7 J Pliekšāna iela) in which he lived with his wife, the poet Aspāzija, from 1927 until his death on September 12 1929. The room in which Rainis worked has been left intact: his books, papers and even the woven blanket which his mother made for him all remain; a similar room contains the remaining effects of his wife. The third room was used by their housekeeper. Open Wednesday to Sunday 11.00–18.00. Admission Ls0.50. Note too the monument to Rainis and Aspāzija on Jomas iela next to the Jūrmala culture centre; erected in 1990 it is the work of the sculptors Z Fernava-Tiščenko and J Tiščenko.

Also nearby is the **Aspāzija House** (18/20 Meierovica prospekts, Dubulti; tel: 776 9445), where Aspāzija (1865–1943) lived the last ten years of her life. It is a small summer cottage, typical of wooden seaside architecture of the early 20th century. Open Monday 14.00–19.00; Tuesday, Wednesday, Thursday, Saturday 11.00–16.00. Admission Ls0.30.

If you are interested in traditional Latvian life, you can visit the **Jūraslīcis Open Air Fishery Museum** (Jūraslīcis brīvdabas muzejs) at Buļļuciems, a modest complex of 19th-century wooden buildings at 1 Tīklu iela (tel: 775 1121). To find the museum watch out for the black anchor on a small pillar of stones, just beyond the Kulturnams in the centre of the village. Tīklu iela takes you to the museum. Open 10.00–18.00. Admission Ls0.50.

Jūrmala

Luckily the **Exhibition of Old Machinery** (11 Turaidas iela, Dzintari, tel: 926 3329) is more interesting than its name implies. It is mainly a collection of old transport (cars, bicycles etc), although there are also some radio sets. One of the exhibits, a motor carriage called 'Victoria', was owned by the Russian tsar Nikolai II and dates from 1907. Open June 1 to August 31 daily 13.00–19.00.

The **Lutheran church at Dubulti**, with its art nouveau elements, plain interior and wooden gallery, used as the Jūrmala Museum of History and Art during the Soviet era, is one of the largest churches in Latvia and its spire is a well-known landmark, visible from the Daugava River. The **Dubulti Orthodox Church** (Sv Kņaza Vladimira pareizticigā baznīca) at 26 Strēlnieku prospekts dates back to 1896 and contains some pleasing icons.

In the early 20th century, Ķemeri was famous for its medicinal mud cures and attracted people from many parts of northern Europe. Like the spa building itself, the **Ķemeri Hotel** is in the classical style. Built between 1933 and 1936 it is known as the 'white castle' or the 'white ship'. The interior is elegant and spacious, the exterior simple yet imposing. The work of E Laube, it ranks as one of the finest examples of architecture from the first period of Latvian independence. The hotel will re-open in 2005 as the Kempinski Kemeri Palace.

Ķemeri National Park

Ķemeri was established as a national park only in 1997. It covers an area of some 40,000 hectares, about 50% of it forest, 30% bog or marshland, 10% water and 10%

agricultural land. About a quarter of all recorded fauna in Latvia can be found here and over half of Latvia's bird species, including the rare sea eagle and black stork. Also to be found here are beavers, which play an important part in the ecology of the area. The park is accessible to the public only by personal application. For further information contact the Information Centre of Ķemeri National Park, Meža Maja, Ķemeri; tel: 773 0078; fax: 773 0207; email: nationalparks@kemeri.gov.lv. To get there take a train to Ķemeri station (see page 195). Alternatively you can take bus number 6 from Sloka or bus number 11 from Lielupe. If you go by car, follow the signs to Jūrmala and continue on the A10 towards Ķemeri.

RUNDĀLE PALACE

Rundāle Palace (tel: 396 2197; fax: 392 2274; email: rpm@eila.lv; www.rpm.apollo.lv. Open daily from 10.00–17.00 from November to April, from 10.00–18.00 in May and September, and from 10.00–19.00 from June to August) is about 77km south of Riga to the west of Bauska and can easily be visited by car or by coach. Consult your hotel or one of the tour organisers mentioned on page 49 for details of coach trips. If you are travelling by car, the road to Rundāle and Pilsrundāle (P103) is signposted on the right after you cross the bridge travelling south over the River Mūsa, leaving Bauska Castle behind you.

If you only visit the palace, a long half-day (four or five hours) would be sufficient. If you combine it with a visit to Mežotne and/or Jelgava, you would need more or less a full day. There is no need to stay in the area, as you can return to Riga easily.

Rundāle Palace

Rundāle Palace

If you wanted to sample life in a Latvian manor house, however, you could overnight at Mežotne.

Rundāle is often billed as the most significant palace in the Baltics. Certainly most visitors will be impressed by its grand exterior, dominating the surrounding flat farmland leading down to the Lielupe River, and the 40 or so sumptuously decorated rooms which have been restored.

Rundāle Palace (Rundāles Pils) was built in the 18th century as a summer palace for Ernst Johann von Bühren (Biron in Latvian) by the Italian architect Francesco Bartolomeo Rastrelli. Rastrelli, already established as the architect of the Winter Palace in St Petersburg, began work in 1736 and took five years to finish the task. The interiors were mostly completed later, between 1763 and 1768. Among those who worked on them were Italian painters from St Petersburg and Johann Michael Graff from Berlin, whose work includes the artificial marble wall panelling and the decorative moulding in many rooms.

Why was such a lavish palace built by Rastrelli beyond the Russian borders? The link with Russia was Anna Ioannovna, a niece of Tsar Peter I who, in 1710, married Frederick, Duke of Kurland. During the 1720s Ernst Johann von Bühren, a Baltic German baron, became her chief adviser, and some say lover also. In 1730, on the death of Peter, Anna became Empress of Russia and delegated much of the management of the empire to a group of German advisers, von Bühren among them. When von Bühren expressed the wish for a summer palace, Anna complied by sending Rastrelli to Kurland and providing all the necessary money and craftsmen too; nearly everyone involved in the construction – a total of 1,500 craftsmen, artists and labourers – was sent from St Petersburg. Before the palace could be finished, however, Rastrelli began work on another major project, a palace at Jelgava, seat of the Duchy of Kurland. Many of the workmen and the materials needed for Rundāle were transported to Jelgava instead. In 1740, just before Rundāle was completed, Anna died, von Bühren was forced into exile, and the building of the palaces halted. Only in 1763 when the Russian Empress Catherine II restored von Bühren to favour, did he return to Kurland and finish the work on Rundāle. The palace was finally completed in 1767, but von Bühren was able to enjoy it for only a short time until his death in 1772. When Russia annexed the Duchy of Kurland in 1795, von Bühren's son, Peter, agreed to leave, taking with him some of the splendid interior items from Rundāle and installing them instead in his properties in Germany. Rundāle itself was given to another favourite of Catherine II, Subov.

Since the incorporation of Kurland into Russia in 1795, the palace has had many uses and owners. Although damaged in the Napoleonic Wars and again during World War II the exterior has been repaired and remains fundamentally unaltered from its original design. The interior has not survived so well. Parts of the castle were used as a granary after 1945, and other areas fell into severe disrepair. In 1972, however, the Rundāle Palace Museum was established and major restoration work began. Artists in Leningrad began the restoration of works of art, and they were subsequently joined by experts from Riga, Moscow and Belarus. As a result the 40 or so rooms (out of 138) restored contain many impressive, but few original, works of art. Particularly interesting are the Golden Hall (the throne room), with beautiful ceiling decoration and chandeliers, the grand Gallery (the banquet room) and the aptly named White Hall (the ballroom), with its intricate stucco. Look out here for the storks! The palace also houses some permanent exhibitions: Treasures of the Rundāle Palace, with furniture, porcelain, silverware and paintings, and 'The Time of Misery', an exhibition about Lutheran churches in Latvia during the years of Soviet power.

Behind the palace, the French-style formal garden has been largely reconstructed. It is surrounded by a canal, beyond which are hunting grounds.

On the south side of the palace is a formal baroque garden, still being reconstructed. A restaurant in the palace is used for formal receptions, and is a favourite place for weddings.

From Rundāle Palace

If Rundāle gives you a taste for Latvian history, you might like to combine your trip here with a stop at **Mežotne** (contact Mežotne pils, Mežotnes pag; tel: 396 0711; fax: 396 0725; email: mezotnpils@apollo.lv), a classical manor house, 10km from Bauska, built between 1797 and 1802 for Charlotte von Lieven, the governess of the grandchildren of the Russian empress Catherine II and an ancestor of the journalist, Anatole Lieven. The rooms on the second floor have been restored and are generally open for visits daily, except Saturday and Sunday, between 10.00–17.00. A hotel was opened in the manor house in August 2001. Prices are Ls30 for singles, Ls40–45 for doubles.

Another possibility for the same trip is a visit to the family vault of the dukes of Kurland at **Jelgava Palace** (tel: 300 5617). The palace is on the eastern side of the town on the Riga road at the end of Lielā iela on a small island in the Lielupe River, and very close to the Jelgava Hotel. Like Rundāle – and for the same reasons – Jelgava palace was built in two phases by Rastrelli, 1738–40 and 1763–72, for the use of Ernst Johann von Bühren. The vault contains 21 metal sarcophagi and nine wooden coffins, with members of the House of Kettler and the von Bühren family entombed between 1569 and 1791. A display in the vault contains full details, as does an English guide, *The Family Vault of the Dukes of Kurland*, published by the Rundāle Palace Museum and available at the museum and from the nearby Jelgava Hotel. It is open 10.00–16.00 except Sunday May to October, and except Saturday and Sunday November to March.

SIGULDA AND CĒSIS
Transport
Sigulda and Cēsis can easily be visited in a day from Riga by train, bus or car, or you can take a coach trip. For information about tours, consult your hotel or one of the tour organisers mentioned on page 49. By car, the journey to Cēsis takes around one hour, to Sigulda a little less. There is a good bus service from Riga. From the main bus station in Riga the journey to Sigulda takes one hour. Buses leave every 30 minutes between 7.00 and 21.30. To Cēsis the journey takes two hours, and buses leave at 8.05 (except Sunday), 9.00, 9.30 (except Saturday), 10.00 (except Sunday), 11.00, 12.00, 13.10, 14.00, 15.00, 16.00, 16.45, 18.05, 19.00 and 20.30. There are also regular trains (tel: 583 2134) which tend to take slightly longer than the bus. Train prices are Ls0.71 single to Sigulda and Ls1.10 single to Cēsis.

Accommodation
It is perfectly possible to make a day trip taking in both Sigulda and Cēsis. If you would like to stay overnight, there is a range of possibilities.

Cēsis
Hotel Cēsis 1 Vienības laukums; tel: 412 0122; fax: 412 0121; email: dlg@danlat-group.lv; www.danlat-group.lv.

Located on the main square right in the town centre, this is the best hotel in Cēsis and is a

Danish–Latvian joint venture. Expanded and refurbished in 2000 it now has 41 rooms. It backs on to the Maija Park and is a short walk from the castle. The food in the restaurant is excellent. The staff will arrange sightseeing and tours, car hire, fishing and canoeing. Double rooms cost about Ls42 a night.

Katrīna 8 Mazā Katrīnas iela; tel: 410 7700; fax: 410 7701; email: hotelkatrina@apollo.lv
Another good option, this hotel is in an attractively renovated early 20th-century building in the centre. Prices are Ls24 for a single and Ls32 for a double.

Piparini Youth Hostel 52–54 Dzirnavu iela; tel: 910 5015
Ideal for budget travellers. Beds cost Ls2–4.

Sigulda

Sigulda 6 Pils iela; tel: 797 2263; fax: 797 1443; email: hotelsigulda@latnet.lc; www.hotelsigulda.lv
This central hotel has been renovated recently and all the rooms are spacious and comfortable.

Aparjods 1 Ventas iela; tel/fax: 790 2455; email: aparjods@aparjods.lv; www.aparjods.lv
Just off the A2 behind a garage, on the right as you approach Sigulda from Riga by car, the Aparjods has 15 rooms at Ls27–50. All rooms have satellite TV and some of the suites have jacuzzis. Aparjods also has a restaurant which is open to non-residents. It serves traditional Latvian food in a setting which echoes a medieval Latvian farmhouse. The food and ambience are excellent and include many local ingredients.

Līvkalns Pēteralas iela; tel: 797 0916; fax: 797 0919; email: livkalns@livkalns.lv; www.livkalns.lv
A small, traditionally built 8-room hotel, attractively situated on the edge of Sigulda close to
the path leading to Peter's Cave. It offers doubles at Ls28, and has a sauna with swimming
pool.

Santa Tel: 770 5271; fax: 770 5278; email: hotelsanta@vide.lv; www.hotelsanta.lv
Off the A2, if you continue past the Aparjods towards the lake, you come to this relatively
new hotel. Attractive and modern, it has a good restaurant, sauna and small pool.

Sigulda

Sigulda is about 53km northeast of Riga (about 45 minutes from Riga). It is an
attractive town which feels spacious and elegant, a centre of historic interest, and
an excellent centre for sporting and outdoor activities. The tourist information
office is close to the station at 6 Pils iela inside the Sigulda Hotel (tel/fax: 797 1335;
email: info@sigulda.lv, www.sigulda.lv). Maps and guides are available. Open:
10.00–19.00.

The main sites of interest in Sigulda are across the River Gauja in the Turaida
area, about 4km from Sigulda station. They include Turaida Castle, Dainu kalns (Folk
Song Hill) next to the castle, Turaida Rose's Grave in the castle grounds, and
Gutman's Cave (Gūtmaņa ala) on the road up to Turaida. In Sigulda itself are Sigulda
Castle ruins, the bobsleigh track and Krimulda Castle ruins.

To visit Turaida, go up the hill leading away from the river valley and past the
caves to a car park on the left and opposite it is the entrance to the **Turaida**

Museum Reservation (tel: 971 0402; fax: 297 1979; email: turaida@lis.lv). The reservation is a large park of about 45 hectares through which a series of paths leads you to Turaida's monuments and attractions. It is open from 10.00–17.00 and 09.30–18.00 in the summer months;

The earliest reference to Turaida is in 1207. Albert, the Bishop of Riga, ordered a stone castle to be built here in 1214 to replace a former Liv-built wooden fortress. In the 15th century the Livonian Order took Turaida Castle and adapted it to firearms, but it was recaptured in 1487 and remained under the control of the bishopric until 1561 when Livonia fell to the Poles. In the 18th century, by which time Turaida had lost its military significance, part of the castle was demolished and the materials were used in other buildings, notably the manor house. In 1776 the castle was destroyed again by fire, and only portions of the walls survived. Restoration work began in the 1950s. The original stone castle had high stone walls and five towers. The main tower, from which there is a wonderful view of the Gauja valley on clear days, and large sections of the castle walls have now been restored.

Between the entrance to the reservation and the castle, just above the footpath, you can see the so-called church mound with its wooden church. Inside there is a baroque altar and some beautifully carved wooden pews. The church was formerly surrounded by a traditional cemetery. Now only one grave remains, that of the legendary Maija, the 'Rose of Turaida'. The grave is a common visiting place for newly-weds, partly because of its romantic associations, partly because it is customary in the Baltic states for newly married couples to visit some cultural monument. Fundamentally, however, the story of the Rose of Turaida is a grim one, that of a young woman who chose death rather than enforced marriage or rape.

Behind the church on a hill lies the **Folksong Hill** or **Sculpture Park** known as **Dainu kalns**. Dedicated in 1985 to Krišjānis Barons to mark the 150th anniversary of his birth, it is the setting for a number of works by the Latvian sculptor Indulis Ranks, each one depicting an aspect of Latvian folklore from the *daina* folk songs which Barons collected. Although the folk-song tradition in Latvia is very ancient, it was only in the 19th century that the National Awakening Movement revived interest in it. Krišjānis Barons spent a summer in Sigulda and Turaida, and often walked on the hills close to Turaida Castle, hence the site of the park. The sculptures do not refer directly to particular songs or legends, but rather allude to them in a general way.

If you leave Sigulda by car via Gaujas iela and the bridge you come to the Turaida road (Turaida iela). There is a car park on the right as you drive (or walk) from Sigulda to Turaida. The paths on the other side of the road (a tunnel runs under the road from the car park) lead to an open area where there are several famous caves.

Gūtman's Cave (Gūtmaņa ala), Latvia's largest cave, is 18m deep, 12m wide and 10m high. Located at the base of Taurētāju kalns (**Horn Blower Hill**), a hill used by the Latgals as a lookout post against invading enemies, the cave is actually a grotto that was eroded by a small underground spring and the waters of the Gauja River before the river changed its course by almost half a kilometre at the end of

THE MOUNTAINEER

Then friends depart, first one and then the other,
And solitude grows with each passing year.
Now no companion walks with you like a brother,
No hillside flower blooms to bring you cheer.

The peak is lost in mountain height,
Eternal stillness turns your heart to stone.
No place remains for rest or for respite
A shield of ice entombs your soul like ore,
While earthly longing burns in flesh and bone.

Jānis Rainis (1865–1929)

the 18th century. The water in the cave is said to have magical powers, bringing health and happiness to those drinking it. The name of the cave comes from the German Gutman, either the name of a real person or the German for a good man who is rumoured to have lived in the area and healed the sick with the aid of water from the cave. The walls are covered with countless inscriptions, the oldest dating back to 1668.

Back in Sigulda itself, at 16 Pils iela, the ruins of Sigulda Castle (or Castle of

THE ROSE OF TURAIDA

The story of Maija goes back to 1601 and the Polish–Swedish Wars. Turaida was under siege from Swedish troops who had penetrated into the Gauja valley. After three days of fighting, the Poles were defeated and the castle fell into the hands of the Swedish troops. After the battle, the clerk of the castle was wandering around the battlefield, looking for wounded soldiers. He came across a young girl and took her home with him, naming her after the month of May, the month in which the battle ended and the girl was found. The young girl grew up into a beautiful woman, attracting a great deal of attention from the men of the area. However, the man to whom she was attracted was Viktors Heils, the gardener of the castle. She would observe Viktors from a cave where he and she often met.

Unfortunately for the couple, two Polish army deserters, Adams Jakubovskis and Pēteris Skudrītis, had taken up residence in Turaida and Jakubovskis had also fallen in love with Maija. He began to press Maija to marry him, but she turned him down. With the help of his fellow soldier, Jakubovskis planned to abduct the girl: they sent her a letter, purportedly coming from Viktors asking

Knights of the Sword) which have now been partly restored are worth a visit if time permits. This was the first stone castle to be built outside Riga and dates back to her to come and meet him at the Gutman Cave on August 6 1620. When she arrived at the cave, the two Poles blocked her exit. Maija resisted the advances of Jakubovskis who tried to force himself on her, tearing her clothes. To distract him, Maija said she would give him the scarf she was wearing around her neck (a gift from Viktors): she claimed it had magic properties, and could protect its wearer from an enemy sword. To prove it she invited him to attack her with his sword. Believing her, Jakubovskis struck a blow to Maija's neck, severing her head from her body. The two Poles fled the town.

That night Viktors found her body. Unfortunately for him, an axe (or in some versions of the story a knife) belonging to him was found in the cave, and before long he was charged with murder and found guilty. However, just before he was due to be executed, a repentant Skudrītis returned to the town and told the true story of Maija's capture and how she had procured her own death rather than betray her lover. Jakubovskis had been so horrified at the girl's self-inflicted death that he had hanged himself. Viktors was released, buried his beloved, and planted a lime tree on her grave. A tree still grows on the grave, although it is now old and deformed as a result of a fire in 1972.

1207–26, but was largely destroyed during the Great Northern War at the beginning of the 18th century.

Activities

Just off Gaujas iela, J Poruka iela leads to the Sigulda boarding point of the **cable car** across the Gauja valley to Krimulda. It departs every hour on the hour between 10.00 and 12.00 and then every half-hour until 18.30 and takes you at a height of 80m across the Gauja River valley from Sigulda to Krimulda. You can also go **bungee jumping** from near the cable car (price Ls15 per jump; Ls13 for second jump). It is generally possible from May to October on Saturdays and Sundays from 18.30, but it is best to check (tel: 644 0660; www.lgk.lv). On the Krimulda side of the valley you can visit the ruins of Krimulda Castle. The old Teutonic castle of Krimulda was built between 1255–73 and was used as a residence for visiting dignitaries. It was destroyed in the early 17th century and little of it remains today.

One of Sigulda's most famous sights is the tower of the artificial **bobsleigh run** which plunges into the Gauja valley, one of only 13 in the whole world. It was built in 1986 by Yugoslav engineers and was used by the Soviet bobsleigh team for training. It is 1,420m long and can be visited (generally open 12.00–17.00 on Saturdays and Sundays, but check opening times by calling 797 3813) and used. Amateurs can use a sort of rubber raft instead of a real sleigh; it holds six people and can reach a speed of 60km/h. Rides cost Ls3 per person.

Boat trips on the river and canoeing can be arranged through Makars Travel Agency (2 Peldu iela; tel: 924 4948; fax: 797 0164; email: janis@makars.lv; www.makars.lv). Prices range from Ls4 per person for an hour's boat ride to Ls39 for a three-day canoe trip camping en route.

Cēsis

The small town of Cēsis lies in the centre of the Gauja National Park, about 90km northeast of Riga. Although its population is only about 20,000, it is one of the oldest and prettiest towns in Latvia, and in 2006 will be celebrating its 800th anniversary. Its winding streets, castle ruins and gardens make it a favourite spot for painters. It is also famous for its beer: the Cēsis brewery has been a feature of the town for many years. The tourist information centre is located at 1 Pils laukums (Castle Square) (tel: 412 1815; fax: 410 7777; email: info@cesis.lv).

All Cēsis's attractions can be seen on foot. They include the Stone Castle, Latvia's best-preserved castle ruins, the New Castle, St John's Church and a number of attractive old houses.

The town centre is an open square (Vienības laukums) from which the main streets radiate. If you walk down Lenču iela there is a small park on the right. Turn left into the cobblestone road which leads to the old and new castles. The **New Castle** (which dates from the 18th century) is a pink building with a white tower and the former seat of the Sievers family. Now it houses the **Cēsis Museum of Art and History** (open daily 10.00–17.00). Near the entrance a recent monument commemorates those who suffered

Cēsis Castle

and died during the period of 'Communist terror', 1940–91. The tower offers a panoramic view of Cēsis. Next to it are the ruins of the **Stone Castle** (11 Pils laukums, tel: 412 2615), one of the most impressive fortresses built by the Livonian Order in the whole of the Baltics. It dates from the 13th century and can be visited in daylight hours. The park below it, which was laid out in 1812, has a small lake and fountain. If you make your way around the castle you come to Lielās Kātrīnas iela. The house at number 14 is the one in which Andrejs Pumpurs (the author of the *Lāčplēšis* epic) lived and worked. If you continue along the street you come to Jāṇa baznīca, **St John's Church**, 8 Lielā Skolas iela (tel: 412 4448). The church was built in the late 13th century and was the Dom Church of the Livonian Order. It has many tombs of members of the order, priests and knights, and one of the best organs in Latvia. It is possible to visit the tower for a charge of Ls0.50.

The old centre of the town is a **conservation area**. The main street, Rigas iela, is full of historic buildings. Number 7 Rigas iela is the former town hall and guardhouse (built in 1767); 16 Rigas iela is a medieval guildhall (1788); the former music and singing club, the Harmonija building, is at number 24 – it dates from the early 18th century and now houses a museum dedicated to the composer Alfreds Kalniņš (1879–1951); and the Princešu nams (a house also dating from the early 18th century) is at number 77. The Maija Park was established in the 1800s by the grandfather of the poet Eduards Veidenbaums (1867–92). Veidenbaums was born in Cēsis and is buried in the nearby Liepa cemetery. There is a museum dedicated to his life at 'Kalači', Liepa (tel: 419 5309), a simple house containing manuscripts and other items.

Cēsis is also credited with being the city where the Latvian national flag was created. According to legend, Latvian troops seeking to repel foreign invaders lost their chieftain on the battlefield. They wrapped the dying man in a white flag captured from the enemy in a previous battle. The Latvian warriors gathered around their dying leader who told them they must continue to defend their homeland and drive the enemy away. His body was removed from the flag which was soaked in blood everywhere except the centre where the chief had lain. Enraged by his death, his warriors tied the maroon and white flag to a spear, attacked the invaders, and drove them from their land. Chronicles mention 1279 as the date when this event occurred. The flag was banned during the period of the Soviet occupation. Cēsis was the first city in Latvia to fly it again in 1987.

In the Museum Garden, 9 Pils iela, is a forge for making **traditional jewellery** (Seno Rotu Kalve; tel: 915 8436; email: daumants@softhome.net; www.kalve.times.lv), run by Daumants Kalniņš, a well-known authority on ancient Latvian art. Visitors can watch jewellery being made according to traditional techniques, learn about the history of Latvian jewellery, and can even participate in the process, and of course purchase brooches, bracelets and other items.

SALASPILS

To reach Salaspils by car take the A6 south towards Ogre and look out for the large granite sign 'Salaspils 1941–44'. Take a train heading southeast for Ogre, Lielvārde or Aizkraukle and alight at the Dārziņa stop. A single ticket costs Ls0.28. Then follow the footpath for about 15 minutes. The tourist office advises that visitors should not walk this footpath alone.

First mentioned as a settlement in 1186 it is a place associated with war, death and destruction. The battle of Salaspils of 1605 delayed the Swedes from gaining a foothold in Latvia. Some 12,000 Swedes under the leadership of Charles IX attacked a Lithuanian unit of about 4,000 men but were repulsed: only about a quarter of the Swedish army managed to retreat to their ships in Riga.

Now, however, it is remembered largely as the site of the Nazi concentration camp, Kurtenhof. Built in 1941 during the Nazi occupation of Latvia in World War II, the camp operated for three years. In 1944, as the Red Army approached Riga, the camp guards and administrators ordered the inmates to exhume and burn the thousands of bodies buried at the camp; it then was burnt to the ground by the retreating Nazis in an attempt to hide the atrocities committed there. Over 100,000 men, women and children, most of them Jews, were put to death here, among them Austrians, Belgians, Czechs, Dutch, French, Latvian, Polish and Soviet citizens. Today, lines of white stones mark the perimeter of the camp.

The Salaspils memorial, which now dominates the site of the former camp, was erected in 1967 to honour those who died there. A huge concrete wall in the shape of a long beam marks the position of the former entrance; symbolising the border between life and death, it bears the words of the Latvian writer, Eižēns Vēveris (a prisoner at Salaspils): 'Aiz šiem vārtiem vaid zeme' ('Beyond these gates the earth moans'). You can actually walk the length of the wall on the inside – there is a door at each end. A series of steps takes you through a number of gloomy rooms, giving the impression of a mausoleum. There is also a small exhibition with photographs of the camp. The seven sculptures which stand in the grounds behind the wall evoke the suffering but also the spirit of defiance and resistance of those imprisoned and killed.

The stillness of Salaspils is broken only by the ticking of an underground metronome beneath the altar-like structure located to the left as you enter the grounds. The noise of the ticking is a reminder of the lives spent and ended here. A narrow path leads through the woods to the place where the prisoners were executed.

12 Language

Latvian is an Indo-European language but bears little resemblance to any language visitors are likely to know. Unfortunately, it is not an easy language to learn. Nouns decline (there are six cases), and the verbs conjugate (there are three conjugations). Even names of non-Latvians are generally Latvianised, by adding 's' to male names and 'a' to female names, for example Tonijs Blērs, Džordžs Bušs and Britnija Spīrsa. A number of grammatical constructions used in Latvian do not exist in English. Although the pronunciation is regular, the intonation is fairly sing-song, and words tend to be run together, making everyday speech difficult to understand without a great deal of practice. The majority of signs are in Latvian only, and the same applies to much of the information in museums and other places of interest.

In Riga, however, English is now widely spoken, and menus are usually available in English, German and Russian as well as Latvian.

It is unlikely that you will have communication problems in Riga. Many people, particularly young people, speak English. However, it is always good to be able to say at least a few basics in Latvian. *Labu laimi!* (Good luck!)

PRONUNCIATION
Consonants

The letters b, d, f, g, h, k, l, m, n, p, s, t, v and z are almost identical to their English counterparts in pronunciation. Other consonants are pronounced as follows:

c as **ts**
č as **ch** in 'chalk'
ġ as the **dj** sound in 'during'
j as **y** in 'yes'
ķ as the **tj** sound in 'Tuesday'
ļ as the **lli** sound in 'million' (or the gl in Italian)
ņ as the **ni** sound in 'onion' (or ñ in Spanish)
š as **sh** in 'show'
ž as s in 'vision'
r is trilled

Vowels

The short and long vowels are:

a as the **o** in 'hot'
ā as in 'father'
e as in 'bet'
ē as the **a** in 'bare'
i as in 'pit'
ī as the **ee** in 'feet'
u as the **oo** in 'foot'
ū as the **oo** in 'food'
The **ai** combination is pronounced as the **i** in 'bike'

The **ei** combination is pronounced as **ey** in '**hey**'
The letter **o** is a diphthong as in the r-less pronunciation of '**pour**'
ie is pronounced as in the r-less pronunciation of '**beer**'

USEFUL WORDS AND EXPRESSIONS
Greetings and courtesies

hello	*Sveiki*
good morning/afternoon; hello	*Labdien*
good morning	*Labrīt*
good evening	*Labvakar*
good night	*Ar labu nakti*
goodbye	*Atā*
goodbye (cf *au revoir, auf Wiedersehen*)	*Uz redzēšanos! Visu labu!*

Basic courtesies

Please	*Lūdzu*
Thank you	*Paldies*
You're welcome (cf *bitte, prego*)	*Laipni lūdzu*
Yes/No	*Jā/Nē*
Excuse me	*Atvainojiet, lūdzu*
I'm sorry	*Es atvainojos* or *piedodiet*
Don't mention it	*Nav par ko*

Basic communication

Do you speak English?	*Vai Jūs runājiet angliski?*
I do not speak Latvian	*Es nerunāju latviski*
Please speak slowly	*Lūdzu runājiet lēnāk*
I do not understand	*Nesaprotu*
Repeat it, please	*Lūdzu atkārtojiet*
Write it down, please	*Lūdzu pierakstiet to*
Wait!	*Pagaidiet!*
My name is...	*Mani sauc...*

Question words and phrases

What?	*Kas?*	When?	*Kad?*
Who?	*Kas? Kuršs?* (m);	How much?	*Cik?*
	Kura? (f)	What time is it?	*Cik pulkstenis?*
Where?	*Kur?*	How?	*Kā?*
What time does it open?		*No cikiem ir atvērts?*	
What time does it close?		*Cikos slēdz?*	

Signs

Closed	*Slēgts*	Parking	*Autonovietne*
Open	*Atvērts*	No parking	*Stavēt aizliegts*
Entrance	*Ieeja*	Stop	*Stāt*

Useful words and expressions

Exit	*Izeja*	Information	*Izziņu birojs*
Pull	*Vilkt*	Ladies	*Sievietēm*
Push	*Grūst*	Gentlemen	*Vīriešiem*
No entry	*Ieeja aizliegta*	No smoking	*Smeķēt aizliegts*
Caution	*Uzmanību*	Petrol	*Degviela* or *Benzīns*
Danger	*Briesmas*		

Finding the way

I would like to go (by car) to...	*Es vēlos braukt uz...*
I would like to go (by foot) to...	*Es vēlos iet uz...*
Where is ...?	*Kur ir...?*
Go straight ahead	*Uz priekšu*
Turn left at...	*Pa kreisi pie...*
Turn right at...	*Pa labi pie...*

Restaurants and meals

See page 72 for more information and vocabulary relating to Latvian food and drink.

breakfast	*brokastis*
lunch	*pusdienas*
dinner	*vakariņas*

Language

restaurant	*restorāns*
café	*kafejnīca*
I would like to order	*Es vēlētos pasūtīt*
Some more, please	*Lūdzu, vēl*
That's enough, thank you	*pietiek, paldies*
hot	*karsts*
cold	*auksts*
Bon appétit!	*Labu apetiti!*
Cheers!	*Priekā!*

coffee (with milk)	*kafija (ar pienu)*
sugar	*cukurs*
tea	*tēja*
juice	*sula*
water	*ūdens*
mineral water	*minerālūdens*
beer	*alus*
wine (red, white)	*vīns (sarkans, balts)*
bread	*maize*
butter	*sviests*
The bill, please	*Lūdzu, rēķinu*
toilet	*Tualete*
	(see also page 43)

Finding a room

Do you have any rooms available?	*Vai Jums ir brīvas istabas?*
I would like a single room	*Es vēlos istabu vienai personai*
I would like a double room	*Es vēlos istabu divām personām*
How much is it a night?	*Cik maksā viena nakts?*
Is breakfast included?	*Vai brokastis ir ieskaitītas?*
bath	*vanna*
shower	*duša*

Useful words and expressions

Shopping

store	*veikals*	expensive	*dārgs*
I would like...	*Es vēlētos...*	open	*atvērts*
How much does it cost?	*Cik maksā?*	closed	*slēgts*
inexpensive	*lēts*	Do you have...?	*Vai Jums ir...?*

Locations

street	*iela*	castle	*pils*
road	*ceļš*	church	*baznīca*
avenue	*avēnija prospeksveits*	restaurant	*restorāns*
square	*laukums*	hospital	*slimnīca*
hotel	*viesnīca*	cinema	*kinoteātris/kino*
drugstore/ pharmacy	*aptieka*	railway station	*dzelzceļa stacija*
theatre	*teātris*	hill	*kalns*
museum	*muzejs*	lake	*ezers*
post office	*pasts*	sea	*jūra*
airport	*lidosta*	river	*upe*
bus station	*autoosta*	bridge	*tilts*

Language

Emergencies

help!	*palīgā!*
quickly	*ātri*
doctor	*ārsts*
dentist	*zobārsts*
pharmacy/chemist's	*aptieka*
hospital	*slimnīca*
police	*policija*
police station	*policijas iecirknis*
telephone	*telefons*
garage (repairs)	*tehniskās apkopes stacija*
garage (petrol)	*degvielas uzpildes stacija*

Days

Note that on signs denoting opening times the days of the week are often expressed as numerals, I denoting Monday, 2 Tuesday etc.

Monday	*pirmdiena*	Friday	*piektdiena*
Tuesday	*otrdiena*	Saturday	*sestdiena*
Wednesday	*trešdiena*	Sunday	*svētdiena*
Thursday	*ceturtdiena*		

Useful words and expressions

yesterday	*vakar*	tomorrow	*rīt*
today	*šodien*		

Numbers

1	*viens*	17	*septiņpadsmit*
2	*divi*	18	*astoņpadsmit*
3	*trīs*	19	*deviņpadsmit*
4	*četri*	20	*divdesmit*
5	*pieci*	25	*divdesmitpieci*
6	*seši*	30	*trīsdesmit*
7	*septiņi*	40	*četrdesmit*
8	*astoņi*	50	*piecdesmit*
9	*deviņi*	60	*sešdesmit*
10	*desmit*	70	*septiņdesmit*
11	*vienpadsmit*	80	*astoņdesmit*
12	*divpadsmit*	90	*deviņdesmit*
13	*trīspadsmit*	100	*simts*
14	*četrpadsmit*	110	*simtdesmit*
15	*piecpadsmit*	1,000	*tūkstotis*
16	*sešpadsmit*	1,000,000	*miljons*

Language

Further information

BOOKS

Visitors wanting to know more about the history of Riga or about its buildings, monuments and parks could not do better than to buy a copy of *Riga for the Curious Traveller* by Andris Kolbergs, translated into English by Anita Liepiņa (AKA, Jūrmala, 2003). The detailed account covers not only central Riga but also the surrounding suburbs and gives a fascinating perspective on the development of the city. If only it had an index!

Riga, The Complete Guide to Architecture by Jānis Krastiņš and Ivars Strautmanis (Add Projekts, Rīga 2004) is an authoritative and well-produced guide to over 700 buildings in and around Riga.

A number of beautifully illustrated and informatively written booklets were produced by the Latvijas Instituts in the run-up to Riga's 800th anniversary in 2001. Titles include *Riga the City of Gardens*, an account of all Riga's parks, cemeteries and gardens, *Latvian Folk Songs*, *The Latvians – a Seafaring Nation*, *Latvian National Costumes* and *Ecotourism in Latvia*. These can be obtained via your local Latvian Embassy or direct from the Latvijas Instituts (1–3 Smilšu iela, Riga, LV-1050; tel: 750 3663; email: instituts@latinst.lv; www.latinst.lv). *The Art Nouveau Architecture of Riga* published in 1998 by the Riga City Council provides a comprehensive pictorial review of the main building styles. Pictures of buildings can also be seen at www.vip.latnet.lv/ArtNouveau.

For a general introduction to the history of Latvia and the early years of independence Anatol Lieven's *The Baltic Revolution* (Yale University Press, 1994) is so far unrivalled. Looking back further to Soviet times, two well-known travel writers have written accounts of journeys in the Soviet Union which include chapters on the Baltic states during the occupation: *Journey into Russia* by Laurens van der Post (Hogarth Press, 1964), and *Among the Russians* by Colin Thubron (Penguin, 1983). A poignant examination of memories of deportation and exile during the Soviet occupation has also been conducted and published by Vieda Skultans in *The Testimony of Lives* (Routledge, 1997).

A good airport read to put you in the mood for a trip to Riga is Henning Mankell's *The Dogs of Riga* (English edition, Vintage, 2002). Although locals claim they can point out inaccuracies in the descriptions of Riga, the novel creates an atmospheric reconstruction of Riga just before independence.

MAPS

All the city guides have maps of central Riga on their back pages. If you need to see all the suburbs, local publisher Jāņa Sēta produces a large number of maps of Riga and the surrounding district, as well as of towns such as Jūrmala, Cēsis, Sigulda and Bauska. You can buy these at the Jāņa Sēta shop (83–85 Elizabetes iela; tel: 709 2288; www.kartes.lv).

WEBSITES

A good general site to start from for general information about Latvia is the Latvian Institute: www.latinst.lv. The site provides fact-sheets on many aspects of life in Latvia, as well as a list of events throughout the year, and a long list of web links to other Latvian sites of interest.

The sites www.latviatourism.lv and www.lv provide more tourist-related information, including details of museums and hotels. The websites for the city guides are kept up to date with information about events and can be accessed at www.rigathisweek.lv and www.inyourpocket.com/latvia/en. The website of Baltic City Papers also provides useful tourist information, news and events listings: www.balticsww.com. Details of museums throughout Latvia, including a comprehensive listing of all museums in Riga, are provided at www.muzeji.lv.

For current news and affairs in Riga and the whole of the Baltic states, try www.baltictimes.com, the website for the English-language newspaper. For the latest weather forecasts for Riga, www.wunderground.com/global/stations/26422.html can help. If you want to know how the economy is going, www.em.gov.lv, the Latvian Ministry of Economy site, is kept up to date. For more details about Riga and its government, consult the municipal site: www.riga.lv.

Index

Page numbers in bold indicate major entries.

Index

Index

Index

Index

242

Index